LEVEL F

Comprehension PLUS

Dr. Diane Lapp
Dr. James Flood

Modern Curriculum Press

Pong® is a registered trademark of Atari, Inc. and parent company Hasbro, Inc. Use of this trademark implies no relationship, sponsorship, endorsement, sale, or promotion on the part of Modern Curriculum Press, Inc.

All photographs ©Pearson Learning unless otherwise noted.

Photographs:
1: Adam Woolfitt/NGS Image Collection. 29: Kwangshin Kim/Photo Researchers. 42(t): Photofest. 42(b): Photofest. 43(t): Archive Photo. 43(b): Photofest. 46: Gene Trind/MPTV. 47: Bernhard Edmaier/Science Photo Library Photo Researchers. 48(l): R.G. Everts/ Photo Researchers. 48(r): Harvey Lyode/FPG International. 51: Jeff Schultz/Alaska Stock/PNI. 52: Associated Press/AP. 53: Archive Photo. 57: Neal Preston/CORBIS. 58: AFP/CORBIS. 60: Najlah Feanny/Stock Boston. 61: Archive Photo. 62: Photofest. 64: Express Newspaper/ Archive Photo. 72: Michael Lutch for WGBH/Everett Collection. 81: CORBIS. 82: 2000 Redding Crew/USDA Forest Service. 85: Danny Kirst/Uniphoto. 86(t): Courtesy of New York Transit Museum Archives. Brooklyn. 86(b): Gail Mooney/ CORBIS. 108: M.P. Kahl/Photo Researchers. 111: S. McBrady/PhotoEdit. 112: Cate Myrleen/PhotoEdit. 123: Sharon and Ray Baily/Uniphoto Picture Agency. 132: AFP/ CORBIS. 134: Manfred Mehlig/Stone. 144(t): Lowell Georgia/ CORBIS. 144(m): Kevin R. Morris/ CORBIS. 144(b); Lowell Georgia/ CORBIS. 146: Jim Sugar Photography/CORBIS. 147: Associated Press/AP. 148: Associated Press/AP. 154(l): Virtual Reality Lab/University of Michigan. 154(r): Virtual Reality Lab/University of Michigan.

Illustrations:
5, 6, 9: Judy Love. 11, 12, 14: John Nez. 15, 16, 17: Judy Love. 25, 26, 28: Wallace E. Keller. 33, 34, 35: John Nez. 41: Wallace E. Keller. 53, 56: Gershom Griffith. 65, 67, 67: Gershom Griffith. 73, 75, 76: Judy Love. 77, 78, 80: Michael Rex. 95, 96: Judy Love. 107, 108, 110: Michael Rex. 115, 116, 118: Michael Rex. 124, 125, 136, 138: Kathleen Kuchera.

Cover art: Photo montage: Wendy Wax. Background: Doug Bowles.

Design development: MKR Design, Inc. New York: Manuela Paul, Deirdre Newman, Marta Ruliffson.

Modern Curriculum Press
An imprint of Pearson Learning
299 Jefferson Road, P.O. Box 480
Parsippany, NJ 07054-0480
www.pearsonlearning.com

ISBN: 0-7652-2185-3

Table of Contents

Comprehending Text

Story Structure

Word Study

Document Reading

Main Idea and Supporting Details

The **main idea** of a story or an article is the most important idea about the topic—the point the writer wants you to understand and remember. In some paragraphs and articles, the main idea is stated in a topic sentence. The topic sentence often, but not always, appears at the beginning of a piece of writing. When you know the main idea, you are much more likely to remember what you have read.

The **supporting details** in a paragraph or article are sentences that tell about or support the main idea. Supporting details are small pieces of information that help you better understand the main idea.

Read the following paragraph. As you read, look for the main idea.

The King Arthur legends are often remembered for their large cast of memorable characters. First is Arthur himself. He was the wise, brave ruler of the Knights of the Round Table. His beautiful queen, Guinevere, is also a favorite of many people. The daughter of a king, she helped Arthur to rule Camelot. Of course, the Arthur legends would not be complete without the brave knights themselves. These noble men give the legends such great heroic characters as Lancelot, who was famous for his skill in combat. Another famous knight, Gawain, was known for his great courtesy.

Underline the sentence that is the main idea of this paragraph.

The King Arthur legends are often remembered for their large cast of memorable characters.

First is Arthur himself.

Of course, the Arthur legends would not be complete without the brave knights themselves.

What details support this main idea?

_____

_____

The main idea of a paragraph or article is not always stated directly. In those cases, you can figure it out. First study the supporting details. Then think of a topic sentence that summarizes the important information in the supporting details.

Read the following legend about King Arthur. As you read, look for the main idea and supporting details.

The king of England had died, and many powerful nobles wanted to be the next king. These lords of the region rode from far and wide to meet in the great city of London. Each was sure he would be the next king. At an inn, the nobles were startled to find a giant stone with a sword embedded in it. Writing on the stone announced that whoever could pull the sword from the stone would be king. One by one, the lords tried, but the sword held firmly. Then Arthur, a boy who had traveled with one of the nobles, stepped forward. In Arthur's hands, the great sword slid out easily! Arthur was crowned king, and he vowed to be a wise and fair ruler.

If the main idea is stated in the paragraph alone, write the word *stated* on the lines provided and circle the topic sentence. If the main idea is unstated, write the word *unstated*. Then write a topic sentence of your own on the lines.

_____

_____

_____

Write two supporting details that helped you figure out the main idea.

1. _____

   _____

2. _____

   _____

Tip

A writer does not always state the main idea of a story or article. You can figure out the main idea by summarizing the information given in the supporting details.

Was There Really a King Arthur?

by Lou Ann Walker

Did a king named Arthur really live in the late fifth or early sixth century? Did he invent the Round Table? Were Guinevere, Lancelot, and the other characters in Arthur's story real people? These questions have captivated historians and writers for centuries. Worthy proof is hard to come by. The events described in legends about King Arthur took place in the Dark Ages. Little was written down during that time. Most of what we know about Arthur comes from poets and storytellers.

When the Romans ruled Britain, beginning in the first century, they built roads and kept order. After they departed early in the fifth century, European invaders arrived. In such chaotic times, people needed inspiration. If the figure of Arthur is purely legendary, it is easy to see why the myth sprang up—and continued growing.

In the 1130s, Geoffrey of Monmouth wrote *History of the Kings of Britain*. Arthur's fame spread. A fanciful writer, Geoffrey said that Arthur fought the Saxons with a sword called "Caliburn." After marrying Guinevere, he brought together knights from every corner of the earth. Later writers further embellished the tale. Sir Thomas Malory, who wrote about Arthur in the late 1400s, was one of the authors who added his own ideas to the story.

In building the case for a real-life Arthur, some people point to the writings of early Welsh historians. A sixth-century writer told of a leader named Ambrosius Aurelianus. This leader fought against the Anglo-Saxons in the fifth century. In the 800s, a Welsh monk wrote of "Artorius." This means "Arthur" in Latin. The monk called Artorius a "leader of battles." Other people who might have been Arthur include a Scottish prince and a Welsh king. One scholar claims that Arthur is Riothamus, a Briton who led an army in A.D. 470. The name means "supreme king." It might have been given to Arthur.

What about Camelot? In the 1960s, archaeologists were studying the ruins of Cadbury Castle in Somerset, England. They uncovered a large hall with a fifth-century gatehouse. The owner must have been extremely powerful, and the site fits in with the area storytellers claim is Camelot.

Is Arthur a historical figure around whom legends grew? Or is he a legendary figure we've tried to make real? We will probably never know for certain. We do know that some of the details of our fantasies, such as knights in armor roaming a grand palace, could not be authentic. Arthur's story comes from the Dark Ages, before armor was invented. More certain is that the Arthurian legend, with all its intrigue, bravery, and chivalry, will continue to fascinate people for centuries to come.

Ruins of Cadbury Castle in Somerset, England

Checking Comprehension

1. What reason might people have had for inventing the stories of the legendary king named Arthur?

   _____

   _____

2. Was Arthur a real figure or an imaginary one? Explain your answer.

   _____

   _____

   _____

Practicing Comprehension Skills

3. Was the main idea of "Was There Really a King Arthur?" stated or unstated?

   _____

4. Write the main idea of "Was There Really a King Arthur?" in the top box. Write a supporting detail in each of the other boxes.

   Main Idea: _____

   _____

   _____

   Supporting Detail:

   _____

   _____

   Supporting Detail:

   _____

   _____

   Supporting Detail:

   _____

   _____

Fill in the circle before the correct answer or answers.

5. Which statement supports the idea that Arthur might have existed?

○ A Welsh monk wrote of a great leader, Artorius, which is Latin for "Arthur."

○ Everyone has heard of King Arthur.

○ There are many movies about the knights of the Round Table.

○ Romans ruled Britain in the first century.

6. What if the following statement had been the main idea of this passage: "King Arthur was an authentic figure of history"? What kinds of details would the author have needed to include to support this statement?

_____

_____

_____

Read the following passage.

During the past century, the King Arthur legend has been retold in numerous books, films, TV shows, and even a major musical. In 1917, *The Boy's King Arthur*, a version of Sir Thomas Malory's tales, was illustrated by artist N. C. Wyeth. T. H. White's *The Once and Future King*, a collection of four novels published together in 1958, brought the Arthur legend to a new generation.

In 1960, the musical *Camelot*, based on White's novel, opened on Broadway. A movie version followed in 1967. Another movie, 1981's *Excalibur*, adapted Sir Thomas Malory's tales, and a television show retelling the legend was the highest rated miniseries in 1998.

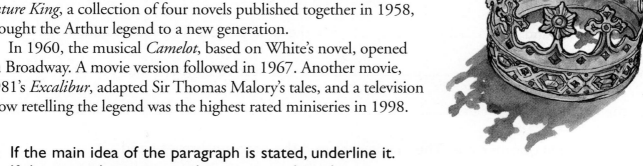

7. If the main idea of the paragraph is stated, underline it. If the main idea is unstated, write it on these lines.

_____

_____

8. Fill in the circle next to the best title for the passage.

○ The Books Inspired by the King Arthur Legend

○ The Legend of King Arthur Lives On in Numerous Retellings

○ Stage and Screen Versions of the Arthur Legend

○ The Story of Arthur and Guinevere

List three details that support the main idea you identified for the passage on page 9.

9. _____

10. _____

11. _____

Practicing Vocabulary

12. Choose the word from the box that best fills each blank in the paragraph.

| authentic | captivated | chaotic | chivalry | embellished | legendary | worthy |

I just saw the new movie about King Arthur, and I was _____ !

It was truly a _____ way to spend a rainy afternoon. The movie showed

how confused and _____ the Dark Ages were. The costumes

looked very real and _____ for the time period. The movie added

some original touches that _____ the stories about Arthur's knights.

Since the characters might be _____ figures rather than real ones from history,

the additions didn't bother me. The movie captured the heroism, bravery, and

_____ of the knights of the Round Table.

Writing a Paragraph
Think of a legendary character from a book or folktale. On a separate sheet of paper, write a paragraph telling what you know about this character. State your main idea clearly in a topic sentence. Then use supporting details to tell more about the character.

Drawing Conclusions

When you read, you often have to draw conclusions about people, places, things, and events. A **conclusion** is a sensible opinion you have or a decision you reach after thinking over the facts or details you've read.

Drawing a conclusion is a two-step process. First, you note the facts and details you have read about a person, place, thing, or event. Then you put that information together with what you know from your own experiences. Asking yourself questions like these will help you draw conclusions:

- What do these details suggest?
- What do these facts mean?
- What do this character's appearance, words, and behavior reveal about him or her?

Read the following story. Then draw some conclusions of your own.

Sylvia stopped in surprise in the doorway of the classroom. Someone new was sitting at the desk right behind hers. The classroom rang with chatter and activity, but the new girl sat alone, quiet and still. She was startled when Sylvia thumped her books down and smiled a greeting. "I'm Sylvia. What's your name?" she asked.

"I'm Emily Ozawa," answered the classmate, smiling back.

"Come meet my friends," urged Sylvia. "I think you'll like them!" She led Emily over to a lively group. By the time the bell rang, Emily felt as if she'd known Sylvia and her friends for years.

What conclusion can you draw about Sylvia after reading the story?

_____

_____

What details support your conclusion?

_____

_____

Tip

Back up your conclusions with information from the text as well as your own experiences with people and events.

Read the following story about an unlikely friendship. As you read, draw conclusions about the characters and events in the story.

Tony's New Neighborhood

Tony shut the front door gently but then stomped down the front steps. He looked around at his new block. Two rows of small, red brick houses faced each other across a narrow city street. Except for an older man sitting on his front steps with a dog at his feet, the block was deserted. "Why did we have to move here?" Tony thought resentfully.

Tony wondered what Sean, Michelle, and José were doing this morning. He looked at the going-away present they'd given him—a baseball signed by several New York Yankees. "I'll never find new friends like them," he thought sadly.

Tony wandered down the street, throwing the ball in the air and catching it. When he missed a catch, the dog sprang up, retrieved the ball, and came running back. The man stood up slowly, leaning on his cane. He wore jeans, a baseball cap, and a faded red shirt. He gently pried the ball from the dog's jaws, grinned at Tony, and glanced at the signatures on the ball as he handed it back. "New York Yankees," he said.

"You like baseball–" Tony hesitated, "sir?"

"Friends call me Cap," answered the man. He sat down again, stretching out his long legs. "I used to play. Then one day I ripped a leg muscle sliding into second base, and it never healed. I had to quit. Are you a pitcher?"

Tony grinned. "I can't hit, so I had to learn to throw. I'm Tony."

"I'm pleased to make your acquaintance, Tony," Cap said formally, shaking hands.

"Just as if I were a grown-up, too," thought Tony. "What's your dog's name?" he asked.

"He's called Joe," Cap answered, "for the day I shook hands with Joe DiMaggio." Joe thumped his tail at the sound of his name.

"You met Joe DiMaggio?" Tony's eyes grew round with wonder.

Cap shifted over on the stoop and Tony sat down, taking off his glove and pushing his hair back. "It was July 1947. My brother Esteban and I had saved our money for a Yankees–Red Sox game. We sat just behind the right field wall.

"When Joe DiMaggio came up in the seventh inning, he smacked the prettiest line drive home run you ever saw—right into my glove! Esteban and I waited after the game and asked Joe to sign the ball for us. I'd heard he was aloof around people, but he was kind to us."

Tony looked at his own prized ball. "My friends saved their money to buy this for me."

Cap took the ball again, turning it around slowly to read all the signatures. Joe pressed his head against Tony's knee. Tony patted the dog. "How about a game of catch?" he asked Cap.

Cap's slow smile wrinkled up the corners of his eyes. "I was just waiting for an invitation."

Checking Comprehension

1. What do you think Tony learned about friendship?

   _____

   _____

2. How is Tony's meeting with Cap like young Cap's meeting with Joe DiMaggio?

   _____

   _____

Practicing Comprehension Skills

Read the questions. Then fill in the circle next to the best answer.

3. How does Tony feel when Cap shakes his hand?

   ○ Tony is angry that he moved away from his friends.

   ○ Tony is afraid of Cap.

   ○ Tony is pleased that Cap shows him respect.

   ○ Tony feels as though he's known Cap for years.

4. Fill in the circle next to the detail that helped you draw the conclusion you did in item 3.

   ○ Tony thinks to himself that Cap is treating him just like a grown-up.

   ○ Cap tells Tony that he shook hands with Joe DiMaggio.

   ○ Tony's eyes grow round with wonder.

   ○ Cap and Tony play catch.

5. How does Tony feel about the going-away present his friends gave him? List some details from the story and something you know from your own experiences that helped you draw this conclusion.

   _____

   _____

   _____

On the chart below, write a conclusion you drew about Cap and Tony's relationship after reading this story. Then list three details from the story that helped you draw that conclusion.

CONCLUSION

6. _____

_____

_____

DETAILS

7. _____

8. _____

9. _____

Practicing Vocabulary

Write a word from the box to complete each sentence.

aloof	formally	pried	resentfully	retrieved	shifted	signatures

10. The catcher _____ his position slightly as he waited for the pitch.

11. Fans complained about the player's _____ manner.

12. The ball sailed over the fielder's head, but he soon _____ it.

13. The girl _____ the ball loose from where it had lodged under the bleachers.

14. Instead of being good sports, the losing team walked _____ off the field.

15. Some autograph collectors get the _____ of famous sports stars.

16. The managers of both teams _____ shook hands before the game.

Write a Story
On a separate sheet of paper, write a short story about a friend. Describe your first meeting. What did you conclude about this person? Try to include specific details about things your friend did or said that helped you draw these conclusions.

Identifying Sequence: Order of Events

Thinking about the order in which events happen helps you understand what you read. The **sequence of events** can be important to the meaning of a story or an article. In many cases, an outcome would change if events had occurred in a different order.

References to dates and times of day are clues to the sequence of events. Words that suggest time order, such as *first, then, meanwhile,* and *next,* or *yesterday, today,* and *afterward,* are also clues.

As you read the following article, look for words that are clues to the sequence of events.

In the American colonies of 1775, no war with England had been officially declared. Massachusetts husbands, fathers, and sons were gathering their weapons anyway. They were preparing to fight for their freedom.

Meanwhile, the British were preparing, too. On April 18, about 700 British soldiers moved toward the town of Concord. They planned to take the colonists' weapons. That same night signal lights flashed in a Boston church. The lights told the colonists that the British were on the move! A few moments later, colonist Paul Revere raced across the countryside. He warned people that the soldiers had been sent to Concord.

The next morning the British were in for a surprise. At the village of Lexington, near Concord, a group of about 70 colonists were waiting.

The events below are out of sequence.
Write numbers from 1 to 5 to show the correct order.

_____ Paul Revere spreads word of the British soldiers' movement.

_____ Colonists store weapons.

_____ Colonists flash signal lights in a Boston church.

_____ An army of colonists surprises the British at Lexington.

_____ British soldiers begin moving toward Concord.

Usually, an author starts a story at the beginning and tells events in the order in which they occurred. Sometimes, however, an author will interrupt the order of events to tell about something that happened before the main action began. This interruption is called a **flashback**.

How can readers tell when a flashback begins? Often an author will use phrases such as *"I remember when . . ."* or *"She thought of the time months ago when . . ."* Such phrases alert readers to the change in time that signals a flashback.

Read this story and look for flashbacks as you read.

The loud knocking woke Isaac from a deep sleep. Who would be out in Lexington at this time of night? Downstairs, Isaac's father opened the door. "The Regulars are out! Be ready!" the stranger announced.

Isaac was thrilled by the news, but not surprised. He remembered how his father had trained with the other patriots last summer. Though father was usually quick with a smile or a witty word, he had taken his training very seriously. Isaac also recalled how, just last week, Father had argued with Sam Collins about the supplies at Concord. "Those weapons will spell trouble for us all," Sam had warned.

Father's boots thumped up the stairs to Isaac's room. "The militia is gathering on the Green, Isaac," he said. "You'll need to take charge at home for a little while."

Read these events from the story. If the incident is part of the main action, write **M** on the line to the left. If the incident is told in a flashback, write **F**. Then, on the lines to the right, number the statements from 1 to 4 to show the order in which they occurred.

_____ Isaac's father trained with other patriots   _____

_____ Isaac's father told Isaac to take charge at   _____
      home for a while.

_____ A stranger came to Isaac's house late at night.   _____

_____ Sam Collins and Isaac's father argued   _____
      about the supplies.

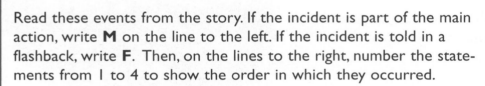

Tip

As you read, try to picture in your mind what is happening. After reading, ask yourself, "Would the outcome have changed if the events had happened in a different order, or if a certain event had not happened?"

Picture events in your mind as you read the following story. Use clue words to keep track of the order in which the events happen.

Redcoats and Homespun

BY BETSY STERMAN

The sound of drums drew Rebecca to the window. Redcoats again, marching out from Philadelphia. What a fine sight!

Rebecca sighed. She ought not to admire the enemy's red jackets, but she couldn't help herself. She looked down at her somber clothes: gray homespun dress, brown shoes laced up over gray stockings. No bright color anywhere—not in this room, and nowhere in the November countryside.

"Rebecca, come away from the window!" her mother called. "'Tis traitorous to look with admiration at the enemy."

"Just their uniforms," Rebecca protested. "They're as fancy as Lucy Wheeler's new shawl."

"Lucy Wheeler is a vain, foolish girl, and the splendid uniforms you so admire are worn by men who war against us."

"I know," Rebecca said, "but I can't help—"

"Can't help giving more notice to what folks wear than to who they are," Mother chided her. "No good will come of such a habit. Now look to your knitting, for Father will need those stockings soon enough."

Rebecca took up her needles. Dear Father. Just yesterday they had received a message from him. He was camped with General Washington's footsore troops northeast of Philadelphia.

A knock sounded at the door. When Mother opened it, there stood a man in farm clothes.

"Looking to join Gen'ral Washington," he said. "Could you spare me something to eat?"

"I can give you some of today's loaf," Mother told him. Rebecca stiffened. Since Washington's defeat at Brandywine, he had moved his troops constantly, hoping to save his poorly equipped men from another battle. Each day, redcoats marched out, searching for him. Spies were busy too, roaming the countryside in various disguises.

She peered closely at the farmer. His knee breeches and jacket were of homespun, his stockings knitted of the familiar gray yarn. A plain countryman, surely welcome in General Washington's weakened army. Still...something about his clothing was wrong. What was it?

As the man leaned back in his chair and stretched his feet toward the hearth, Rebecca's heart jumped. There it was—proof he was no rough countryman, but a spy!

He stood to leave. "Thankee," he said. "Could ye steer me toward Gen'ral Washington...?"

Mother hesitated, but Rebecca blurted, "He's southwest of Philadelphia! Father sent us word!"

After the man was gone, Mother said, "How clever to mislead him, Rebecca. What made you think he was not a simple farmer?"

"Farmers don't wear buckles on their shoes," Rebecca explained.

"Nor did he," Mother said, puzzled. "Plain scuffed shoes he had."

"But with smooth, unscuffed leather where the buckles had been removed!" Rebecca said.

Mother smiled. "Good *does* come of minding what folks wear," she said. Rebecca smiled too. Let Lucy Wheeler have her elegant shawl. Today's adventure made the world bright enough!

Checking Comprehension

1. How does Mother's attitude toward Rebecca and her interest in clothes change from the beginning of the story to the end?

   _____

   _____

2. What causes Rebecca to suspect that the visitor is a British spy?

   _____

   _____

Practicing Comprehension Skills

3. Think about the sequence of events in this story. Write one or two sentences in each box to tell what happened at the beginning, middle, and end of the story.

   Beginning

   _____

   _____

   _____

   Middle

   _____

   _____

   _____

   End

   _____

   _____

   _____

Write answers to the questions on the lines.

4. What are three clue words the writer uses to suggest the time an event occurred?

_____

5. Read the following events from the story. If the event is part of the main action occurring in the present, write M on the line to the left. If the incident occurred earlier and is told in a flashback, write F on the line.

_____ Rebecca gives wrong information to the stranger.

_____ Rebecca's family receives a letter from Father.

_____ A stranger appears at Rebecca's door.

_____ Washington's army is defeated at Brandywine.

_____ Mother bakes a loaf of bread.

_____ Rebecca admires the uniforms of the British soldiers.

6. Reread the six events listed in question 5. Think about the time order in which they occurred. On the time line below, write the events in time order from earliest to latest. Write one event on each set of lines.

Redcoats and **Homespun** TIME LINE

Earliest _____

_____

_____

_____

_____

Latest

7. Which event on the time line is the least important to the story's outcome? Which event is the most important?

_____

_____

8. How would the outcome of this story have changed if Rebecca had answered the stranger's question about General Washington *before* she noticed his shoes?

_____

_____

_____

Practicing Vocabulary

Circle the word or phrase that means the same as the underlined word or words in the sentence.

9. A spy's closet is likely to hold many <u>disguises</u>.

   a. dishes   b. costumes   c. shoes

10. Dark colors are more <u>somber</u> than bright ones.

   a. dull   b. sad   c. simple

11. The stranger seemed to be <u>roaming</u> from one farm to another.

   a. running   b. wandering   c. riding

12. The soldier <u>was footsore</u> after marching 30 miles.

   a. had tired feet   b. was wounded   c. was barefoot

13. Mother <u>chided</u> Rebecca for neglecting her chores.

   a. praised   b. punished   c. scolded

14. After fooling the spy, Rebecca won her mother's <u>admiration</u>.

   a. approval   b. anger   c. surprise

15. The Minutemen were <u>poorly</u> equipped compared to the redcoats.

   a. expensively   b. properly   c. badly

| admiration |
| chided |
| disguises |
| footsore |
| poorly |
| roaming |
| somber |

Writing a News Article

Imagine that you are a reporter covering an important news event. On a separate sheet of paper, write a news story that identifies the events in the order in which they occurred. Use at least two clue words to help your readers keep track of the sequence of events.

Sequence: Steps in a Process

What do a recipe, a model airplane, and a new VCR have in common? All of them come with an organized set of instructions for completing a process. Once you recognize the **steps in a process**, you can use the order of the steps to complete an action.

Before you begin to follow steps in a process, read all the steps carefully. Then you'll have an idea of what you will need to do, and you can gather any necessary materials. Looking carefully at illustrations or diagrams will also make it easier to follow the steps.

Read the following paragraphs. As you read, think about the steps required in the process of planting and growing carrots.

If you're interested in growing carrots, it's important to begin by selecting a bright, sunny spot in your garden. Then you'll need to loosen the soil with a tool called a trowel, which looks like a small shovel. Check to be certain that the soil drains well.

After that, you're ready to plant the seeds. You'll have to be careful as you're planting because carrot seeds are extremely small. Plant them about 1/4 inch deep and 3 inches apart. Gently pat down the soil after each seed is in the ground.

Carrots prefer moist soil. Because of that, it is very important that the soil stays damp until the seeds sprout in 12 to 18 days. As the carrots grow, be careful to keep the soil weed-free. In approximately 60 to 80 days, you can pick the carrots for part of a delicious dinner.

Write these steps in order from 1 to 6:

_____ Plant the seeds.   _____ Locate a sunny spot.

_____ Pick the carrots.   _____ Loosen the soil.

_____ Weed the garden.   _____ Water the seeds.

Write at least three words or phrases that helped you identify the sequence of these steps.

_____

_____

Tip

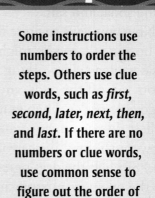

Some instructions use numbers to order the steps. Others use clue words, such as *first, second, later, next, then,* and *last*. If there are no numbers or clue words, use common sense to figure out the order of the steps.

As you read the following recipe, try to visualize what happens at each step and what the final result will look like.

Carrot Cupcakes
by Ann Hodgman

Ingredients

1 1/4 cups corn or canola oil
2 cups sugar
2 cups all-purpose flour
2 teaspoons cinnamon
2 teaspoons baking powder
1 teaspoon baking soda
1 teaspoon salt
4 large eggs, well-beaten
1 pound carrots
1 cup chopped pecans (optional)

If you've been living in an alternate universe and have never tried carrot cake, you may not know how delicious it is. Carrot cupcakes are just as good.

Preheat the oven to 350 degrees. Take 36 cupcake papers and put them into muffin pans. (You may not need all 36, but you can always put the unused ones back.)

In a large bowl, whisk together the oil and the sugar until they're combined. The sugar won't dissolve, but that's okay. In another large bowl, sift together the flour, cinnamon, baking powder, baking soda, and salt.

Now you have to grate the carrots. This is sort of a boring job, so you might want to listen to some music while you're working. Wash the carrots, cut off the ends, and peel them with a vegetable peeler. Then grate them on the smallest side of a metal grater. (Be careful! You want to shred the carrots—not your skin.) Sift half the dry-ingredients mixture into the oil-sugar mixture and beat well. Sift in the second half, beat well again, and then beat in the eggs. Now stir in the grated carrots and the optional pecans, and mix thoroughly.

Using a large spoon, carefully fill the cupcake papers 2/3 to 3/4 of the way. (The batter needs room to rise.) Bake the cupcakes on the middle rack of the oven for 10 minutes. Then—using potholders, of course—rotate the cupcake pans until the back of each is facing front. This will help the cupcakes bake evenly. Bake for 10 more minutes.

Next, choose the most lopsided cupcake and carefully lift it out of the pan onto a plate. Peel off the paper and cut the cupcake in half to see whether it's done. If it is done, take the cupcakes out of the oven. If your test cupcake seems mushy, bake the rest of the cupcakes for another 5 to 7 minutes. (You can't continue baking the bisected cupcake, so if it's done baking, eat it without delay.)

You can ice the cupcakes with your favorite frosting if desired—but let the cupcakes cool *completely* before you ice them. The icing will melt if you put it on while the cupcakes are still hot!

This recipe makes 2 to 3 dozen cupcakes, which you should cover with plastic wrap. The cupcakes will keep at room temperature for at least 3 days. After that, you'll obtain the best results by putting them in the freezer and thawing them as needed—if your family hasn't already devoured them.

Checking Comprehension

1. Aside from the ingredients listed in the recipe, what other things do you need to have on hand in order to make carrot cupcakes?

_____

_____

2. What do you think is the most difficult part about making carrot cupcakes?

_____

Practicing Comprehension Skills

Write your answer on the line.

3. Order these steps to show what happens after you put the cupcakes in the oven. Write the numbers 1–6 to show the correct order.

_____ Then you can eat them.

_____ When they are done, take the cupcakes out of the oven to cool.

_____ After 10 minutes, rotate the pans.

_____ When they are cool, frost them if you wish.

_____ Cover any remaining cupcakes with plastic wrap.

_____ Then, after another 10 minutes, test one cupcake to see if it is done.

4. Between which two steps do you beat in the eggs?

_____

_____

5. Do all of the steps in the recipe have to be completed in the order in which they are listed in the recipe, or can some be switched around? Support your answer with an example.

_____

_____

6. As you read this recipe for frosting, underline all the clue words that help you determine the order of the steps.

First, allow two sticks of unsalted butter and eight ounces of cream cheese to reach room temperature. Then, with an electric mixer, beat the butter and cream cheese together. Next, gradually add four cups of confectioners' sugar, beating well after each addition until the icing is smooth and fluffy. Add one teaspoon of vanilla extract and a pinch of salt, then beat the icing one more time. Finally, spread the icing on the cool cupcakes.

7. Write numbers to show the order of these steps for making icing.

_____ Beat the butter and cream cheese together.

_____ Beat the icing for the last time.

_____ Add vanilla extract and salt.

_____ Allow the butter and cream cheese to reach room temperature.

_____ Spread the icing on the cupcakes.

_____ Gradually add 4 cups of confectioners' sugar and beat after each addition.

Practicing Vocabulary

8. Choose the word from the box that best fills each blank in the paragraph.

alternate	bisected	delay	devoured	ingredients	obtain	optional

I decided to make carrot cupcakes, but first I had to _____ the necessary

_____ . Searching for the cinnamon caused a _____ before I could start

to bake. I decided to skip the _____ pecans and substitute an _____ nut,

walnuts. The first cupcake I _____ was mushy, so I baked the rest for five more min-

utes. My family _____ the cupcakes before I could frost them!

Writing Directions
On a separate sheet of paper, write directions that tell how to prepare something you like to eat. Organize the steps in sequential order and make sure there are at least six steps. Number each step, or use clue words *such as first, next,* and *last.*

Predicting Outcomes

When you read a story or article, you are likely to find yourself making predictions—thinking about what will happen next. Try **predicting outcomes** at several points in your reading. Before you begin, preview the title and pictures to make predictions about what you will read. As you read, use details and your own experiences to predict what might happen next. After reading, check the accuracy of your predictions and think about the clues that helped you predict.

Look at the title and the picture below. Predict what the passage will be about. As you read, use details to predict what will happen next.

THE FUTURE
ALL DEPARTURES
THIS WAY

Ticket to the Future

Bartholomew had ten $20 bills in his pocket and a nervous rumbling in his stomach. He had worked hard to save for the trip to the future. He planned to return home for school in September.

The departure dock was deserted except for the ticket master. Bartholomew bought a ticket printed "For forward travel." The other side had gotten wet, and the lines were blurred. He could make out CAU ON. The word *one* appeared in one line, the word *no* in another.

"All aboard!" cried the ticket master. "Departure time! Now or never!" Bartholomew hurried to the platform.

Once the craft left the station, Bartholomew focused again on the ticket. "Caution!" the heading said. Then, in much smaller print, "For one-way travel only. No return trip."

How did the title or the illustration help you predict what this story would be about?

_____

_____

_____

What clues helped you predict the outcome of this story?

_____

_____

_____

Tip

As you read, look for clues that will help you predict what might happen next. Think about your own experiences and things you have read or heard about.

On Your Own

Use clues in the title and picture to predict what and whom this story will be about. Then read the story. Pause at least once during reading to make predictions.

The New Guy, Ben

The locker swung open, and a boy stepped out and stretched. He smoothed his leather printer's apron, leaving a dark ink splotch.

"It worked," the boy whispered. He moved down the hall, staring intently at the overhead lights. Spying his image in a window, the boy stopped. He straightened his wire-rimmed glasses and smoothed his long, wispy hair as he tucked a kite string back into his pocket.

The boy jumped as a bell sounded. The students of Colonial Heights Middle School swarmed out into the halls.

"Who's the new guy?" asked Patrick.

"Check out the knee pants," said Betsy. "Is he in a rock band? He looks familiar."

One student held out his hand. "I'm Thomas," he said. "And you are . . . ?"

"I'm Ben." When the two shook hands, Thomas was surprised to feel a small electric shock.

As Thomas showed the mysterious visitor around school, the boys discovered they had much in common. Both enjoyed swimming and sailing.

"You would like the place I come from," Ben said, "but I doubt you would enjoy my after-school job."

"I baby-sit after school sometimes so I can buy CDs," said Thomas.

"CDs?" Ben puzzled. "Candle dippers? Copper doorstops?" He said, "I'm saving my wages. After all, a penny saved is a penny earned!"

When Thomas pointed out the library computers, Ben was surprised, but then he got busy at a keyboard. At first he didn't notice the thunder. Then a flash of lightning caught Ben's attention. "Perfect travel conditions," he said, looking wistfully at the computer screen.

Thomas watched Ben from the next computer. On Thomas's screen an encyclopedia entry showed a man with small wire-rimmed glasses. Although the man was balding on top, wispy hair flowed to his shoulders. Dates in the entry read 1706–1790.

"Benjamin," Thomas said gently, "you have to go." He nodded at the flag above the door. "You have things to do. Remind George and Tom J. that we're all created equal. Don't forget the life, liberty, and happiness part."

"It *is* time to go." Ben smiled. "Both fish and visitors smell in three days."

Thomas shook his head. Someone should write a book of this guy's sayings!

A peal of thunder sounded as the boys entered the deserted hall. "Ben," Thomas said, "how did you get here?"

"It's all in the lightning," Ben said. He opened a locker, pushed a kite to the back, and climbed in.

Just one flash glowed from behind the locker door. Thomas knew Ben Franklin was gone.

Checking Comprehension

1. Why does the writer give so many details about Ben, such as his glasses, the kite string in his pocket, and the fact that he comes and goes with lightning?

   _____

2. Thomas tells Ben, "You have to go. You have things to do." What do you think he means?

   _____

   _____

Practicing Comprehension Skills

List three clues from the picture, title, and/or text that helped you predict that Ben was actually the famous Benjamin Franklin from American history.

3. _____

   _____

4. _____

   _____

5. _____

   _____

Complete the following chart by writing on the lines.

What I Already Knew About Benjamin Franklin	What I Predicted Would Happen	What Actually Happened
6. _____ _____ _____	7. _____ _____ _____	8. _____ _____ _____

The following are predictions you might have made as you read the story. On the line after the prediction, write A if the prediction was accurate and NA if it was not accurate. List the clues you could use to check the prediction.

9. The story would involve someone traveling from the past to the future.

_____

_____

10. Ben would bring Thomas back to colonial times.

_____

_____

Practicing Vocabulary

Write a word from the box to complete each sentence.

deserted	familiar	liberty	overhead	peal	wispy	wistfully

11. The school was _____ before the students arrived at 8:00 a.m.

12. We viewed the picture of Ben Franklin on an _____ projector.

13. The thin, _____ clouds were replaced by thick, dark ones.

14. Ben sighed _____ , wishing he could stay a little longer.

15. Ben was used to the musical _____ of bells, but the school bell was a harsh buzz.

16. Ben Franklin helped create the Declaration of Independence, which called for _____ .

17. The name Ben Franklin is _____ to most Americans.

Writing a Journal Entry
Imagine that you are a time traveler visiting America 100 or 200 years in the future. On another sheet of paper, write a travel journal entry describing what you find. Base your predictions about the future on clues you see in the world today.

Recognizing Cause and Effect

Did you ever work hard to make something happen? Maybe you practiced hard in order to perform well at a sport. If so, then you saw **cause and effect** in action. An **effect** is something that happens. A **cause** is the reason it happened. Sometimes one cause can lead to many effects. A bad storm could cause a game to be postponed and also damage homes and flood roads. In the same way, one effect can have many causes. If your team wins, the win may be the result of hard work from you, your teammates, and your coach.

When you read stories and articles, you may stop to think about what happened and why it happened. Clue words such as *because, since, thus,* or *as a result* often signal a cause and effect relationship. If an author doesn't use clue words, ask yourself, "What happened? Why did it happen?"

Read the following story. Think about the cause-and-effect relationships that occur.

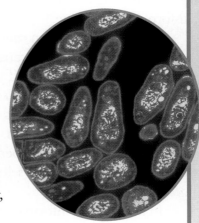

"Class, please don't forget that your research paper is due Monday," my science teacher said.

"Uh-oh," I thought. "Research paper! I completely forgot! Okay, don't panic. There's plenty of time before Monday."

As soon as I got home, I logged on the Internet and started a search. I typed B-I-O-L-O-G-Y in the search window. Wow—it returned thousands of Web sites with the word *biology*! Since that didn't work, I tried to narrow my search. That was a much better idea! We'd been studying germs, so I typed B-A-C-T-E-R-I-A in the search window. Then I got a list that was a lot shorter, but still had several thousand hits! This was going to be harder than I thought.

Fill in the missing causes and effects below.

Cause	Effect
_____ _____ _____	The student began an Internet search.
The student did a search on the word *bacteria*.	_____ _____

> ## Tip
> Clue words such as *because* or *as a result* signal cause-and-effect relationships. When an author does not use clue words, you should ask yourself, "What happened? Why did it happen?"

Read the following article. Pay attention to causes and effects, especially multiple causes or multiple effects.

Traveling on The Information Superhighway

In the early 1990s, few people outside of governments and universities had ever heard the term *Internet*. The World Wide Web was in its infancy. Back then if you said to someone, "Send me an e-mail with directions to your house," all you would have received is a puzzled look. Technology has come a long way since those days. Today, the Internet connects millions of computers around the globe, making a worldwide exchange of information possible.

The Internet is often called the "information superhighway." That's because vast amounts of information travel over it. If you searched the word *grasshopper*, for instance, you would have thousands of sites to look at. Some sites would give information on these insects. Other sites would be companies with "grasshopper" in their names. Still other sites might want to sell you books about grasshoppers.

In addition to information, the Internet also offers one of the greatest inventions in communications: electronic mail, or e-mail for short. E-mail is the brainchild of a shrewd man named Ray Tomlinson. He developed the program and sent himself the first e-mail in 1971. He isn't sure, but he thinks his first message was QWERTYUIOP (the top row of letters on a keyboard). As a result of Tomlinson's invention of e-mail, the way in which the world communicates has changed.

Thanks to e-mail, you can communicate with a student in London and find out how his weather experiment is going. E-mail has also changed the speed with which we exchange information. In minutes, you can contact another person who shares your love of kites or stamps. Your aunt and uncle can send you pictures of their new puppy without ever leaving their home. If you're sick and can't attend school, your teacher can e-mail you the assignments you have missed. You can even send e-mail to a grasshopper expert and ask questions for a research paper.

However, if you're going to use e-mail, you need to follow some simple rules of "Netiquette." Netiquette is the good manners, or etiquette, you should remember when using the Internet. This is especially important when using e-mail. For example, it's rude to shout your e-mail message. How do you shout e-mail? TYPING YOUR MESSAGE IN ALL CAPITAL LETTERS is shouting. It may offend the person you send the message to.

There is one big disadvantage to using e-mail. Unlike a letter you send through the mail, e-mail is NOT private. It can be reviewed by anyone with access to your receiver's computer. Your receiver could also forward it to other people—so be careful. Do not say anything in an e-mail that you wouldn't say in front of a crowd!

Mail Folder "Inbox"		
Subject	From	Received
Math Homework	surfer@xyz.com	7:00 P.M.
My Party	raffles@sunshine.net	5:01 P.M.
Hi From Grandma	ericapatrick@anytown.com	11:46 A.M.

Mail

Checking Comprehension

1. How has the Internet changed our world?

   _____

   _____

2. How is e-mail similar to and different from the postal service?

   _____

   _____

Practicing Comprehension Skills

This article presents several cause-and-effect relationships. Think about the article as you look at the chart below. Where there is a cause listed, write the effect. Where an effect is listed, write what caused it to happen.

Cause	Effect
3. _____ _____	A worldwide exchange of information is possible.
4. Search the word *grasshopper*	_____
5. Type an e-mail message in all capital letters	_____
6. _____	Find yourself embarrassed by an e-mail you sent.

7. What is the cause in this sentence? What is the effect? What clue words helped you to identify the cause and effect relationship?

   As a result of Tomlinson's invention of e-mail, the way in which the world communicates has changed.

   Cause: _____

   Effect: _____

   Clue word or words: _____

Complete this cause/effect sentence.

8. The Internet is often called the "information superhighway" because

_____

List three effects of the invention of e-mail.

9. _____

10. _____

11. _____

Practicing Vocabulary

Write the word from the box that answers each question.

brainchild	infancy	Internet	reviewed	shrewd	sites	technology

12. What are the places on the Internet that have information on a given subject?

_____

13. In what category could you group computers, cell phones, pagers, and VCRs?

_____

14. What do you call it when you have looked at something again? _____

15. What is the name for the "information superhighway" we have today? _____

16. What is another name for someone's idea, invention, or discovery? _____

17. How can you describe an early stage of childhood? _____

18. When someone is very clever, what might you say he or she is? _____

Writing a Persuasive Paragraph
Imagine that your local library does not have enough computers to meet its Internet access needs. On another sheet of paper, write a paragraph to persuade the library to invest in more computers. Be sure to include some convincing cause-and-effect relationships in your paragraph.

Using Context Clues

When you come to an unfamiliar word in your reading, you can use **context clues** to help you figure out its meaning. Context clues may be in the same sentence as the unknown word, or in surrounding sentences. This chart gives examples of four types of context clues.

Definition or Explanation	Example	Synonym	Description
The *slate*, or list of candidates, includes students from every class.	Our president has many fine *characteristics*, such as confidence and friendliness.	The students called for *reforms*. They said changes were needed.	The *incumbent* president had already been in office for a full term.
• The meaning of the word *slate* is explained with a definition.	• *Confidence* and *friendliness* are examples of characteristics.	• The words *reforms* and *changes* are synonyms.	• Context clues describe *incumbent* as someone who is already in an elected position.

Read the following passage. Use context clues to figure out the meanings of the underlined words.

Tanya frowned as her father tossed a tuna can into the trash. She believed everyone ought to recycle, or put items back into use.

Tanya began a family campaign. She made posters and wrote slogans such as, "Use it once, use it twice. Please help make this planet nice!" No one listened, so Tanya quietly began collecting her family's recyclables in a storage closet. A few weeks later Tanya's mother pulled the closet door ajar and gasped. "Where are our suitcases?" she asked.

"They're buried in all this rubbish," Tanya said. "If we don't start recycling, *we're* going to be buried in garbage, too!"

Find each word below in the passage. On the line next to the word, write its meaning. Then write *definition*, *example*, *synonym*, or *description* to name the type of context clue given in the passage.

recycle: _____

slogans: _____

rubbish: _____

ajar: _____

Tip

If the context does not give you a complete or exact meaning, check the unfamiliar word in a dictionary.

On Your Own

Read the following story. Use context clues to figure out the meaning of unfamiliar words.

The Cookie Campaign

The students at Lincoln Middle School looked forward to election time. It meant free stuff! Last year a candidate handed out pens. Another office seeker gave away yo-yos. It was no surprise that the students showed little interest in *who* was running for student government but a lot of interest in *what* a candidate was giving out!

A week before election day, Andy pulled cookies from the oven. Each one had an "A+" formed from chocolate chips. That was Andy's logo, the symbol of his campaign for president. His motto was, "Lincoln gets an A+ with Andy!" He had made chocolate chip cookies, fudge cookies, and brownies. Anyone who loved chocolate would surely vote for Andy.

The same day, Connie left the bakery with boxes full of sugar crinkles and snickerdoodles. She'd spent her savings, but it would be worth it when she was elected student body president.

All that week, Connie and Andy distributed treats. By Friday, the cookie campaign had reached the whole student body. Students were arguing about cookie flavors. They were taking sides—chocolate versus vanilla!

Election day arrived, and just in time! The students had gained a combined total of 500 pounds. Three candidates sat on the stage that day. Few students had realized there was a third student in the race for president. While Andy and Connie had been busy with cookies, Harrison had quietly built his campaign platform. This list of plans was all that Harrison had to offer.

Andy spoke first. He called for a larger dessert selection at lunch. Then his campaign manager served brownies.

Connie moved to the podium. Speaking from the stand, she promised a bigger budget for party refreshments. "We'll have more money available to buy baked goods!" she said.

Finally, Harrison stood. He had no cookies—no gifts at all. "Fellow students," he began, "this cookie campaign has been counterproductive. Rather than producing real ideas, it has led us nowhere. Now, don't think I'm antisocial. I like parties, treats, and good times as much as anyone else does, but there are more important issues for our school to tackle."

The audience put down their cookies and listened as Harrison suggested new programs. He said students could tutor, or teach, classmates after school. Work parties could clean up the ball fields. Harrison had no cookies, but he had ideas.

That election day was a turning point. Oh, everyone still enjoyed a good cookie once in a while, but now the students had advantages such as clean school grounds and volunteer tutors. Led by Harrison, their new president, the chocolate lovers and vanilla fans set aside their differences and addressed real issues. They joined forces to make Lincoln Middle School a better place for all.

Checking Comprehension

1. How was Harrison's campaign different from those run by
    Andy and Connie?

    _____

    _____

2. How do you think Lincoln Middle School's presidential campaign
    might be different next year?

    _____

    _____

Practicing Comprehension Skills

Find each word in the passage. Use context clues to figure out the
meaning. Then fill in the circle before the correct meaning.

3. A logo is a

    ○ catchy saying.　　○ campaign promise.　　○ special symbol.　　○ list of candidates.

4. A podium is a

    ○ candidate.　　○ type of cookie.　　○ voting booth.　　○ speaker's stand.

5. Counterproductive means

    ○ leading
    nowhere.　　○ making a product.　　○ a counter
    for cookies.　　○ producing
    results.

6. Antisocial means

    ○ against dancing.　　○ against the company
    of others.　　○ against food　　○ against the
    issues.

Find each word in the passage. Use context clues to understand the word's meaning.
Then write an original sentence that includes the type of context clue requested
(definition, synonym, example, or description).

7. motto (definition)

    _____

8. addressed (synonym)

_____

_____

9. advantages (example)

_____

_____

10. budget (description)

_____

_____

Practicing Vocabulary

Write a word from the box to complete each sentence.

antisocial	candidate	counterproductive	distributed	platform	tutor	versus

11. The race was Andy _____ Connie until Harrison appeared on the scene.

12. The homeroom teachers _____ ballots to the students.

13. "Complaining can be _____," said the president, "so let's take action and improve our school."

14. That student has an interesting _____ that includes exciting new programs.

15. Although Harrison enjoys time alone, he is very friendly and not at all _____ .

16. The math _____ helped Connie prepare for the final test.

17. The _____ with the best ideas is likely to win the election.

MAKING THE
Reading
AND
Writing
CONNECTION

Writing a Campaign Speech

Imagine that you are running for president of your class, school, club, or other organization. Write a short speech giving reasons voters should elect you. Be sure to check your speech and provide context clues for any words that might be unfamiliar.

Comparing and Contrasting

When you read, you'll find that authors often make **comparisons** that tell how two or more things are alike. They also make **contrasts** that point out differences between the things. Authors compare and contrast so that readers can understand ideas clearly. Sometimes, though not always, authors use clue words such as *like, similar to,* or *also* to compare. Clue words such as *but, different from, however, in contrast,* or *unlike* may be used to show contrasts.

As you read, look for the author's comparisons and contrasts. Also look for ways to make comparisons and contrasts on your own.

Read the following paragraphs. Find comparisons and contrasts.

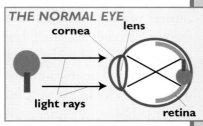

In normal eyes, light rays focus on the back of the eye. This part of the eye is called the retina (RET-in-uh). If your eyes are either nearsighted or farsighted, however, then the light rays do not meet where they should.

Nearsightedness means that close things appear clear but faraway ones look fuzzy and unclear. The eye tends to be too long. The light rays meet before they reach the retina. The image on the retina is then out of focus.

Farsightedness is the opposite problem. Faraway things appear clearer than close ones. The eye is too short, so light rays from close objects are not yet focused when they reach the retina.

Wearing glasses or contact lenses can solve both of these problems.

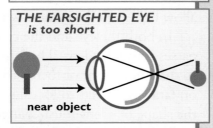

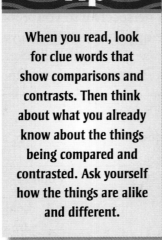

On the chart below write two ways that nearsightedness and farsightedness are alike and two ways in which they are different.

Nearsightedness and Farsightedness

Alike	Different
1. _____ _____ _____	1. _____ _____ _____
2. _____ _____ _____	2. _____ _____ _____

Tip

When you read, look for clue words that show comparisons and contrasts. Then think about what you already know about the things being compared and contrasted. Ask yourself how the things are alike and different.

Read the following article. Think about what is being compared and contrasted, and why.

The Eye and the Camera

How does the human eye see? In some ways, the way you see can be compared to the way a camera takes a picture.

The first thing that an eye needs to see, and a camera needs to take pictures, is light. Light enters the eye through the small hole called the pupil. Around the pupil is the iris, the ring that gives your eye its color. The iris automatically opens or closes the pupil to let in more or less light. In the same way, the hole in a camera, called the aperture, can change size automatically.

Imagine if you had to close your eyes every time you saw something new. A camera is like that. Unlike the eye, a camera must return to darkness right after allowing light to enter. That's why it has a shutter. A camera's shutter acts like a curtain to allow light into the camera when a picture is taken.

In both the eye and the camera, light then passes through a lens. The lens bends the light rays so that they meet, or focus. To shift from focusing on faraway objects to focusing on nearby objects, the shape of a lens must change.

Your eye muscles do this work for you. Try looking at something far away. Quickly change your perspective so you're looking at something close up. Thanks to your eye muscles, the lens of your eye just became thicker. Similarly, the lens of a camera can be changed. One lens might be used for a close-up photograph and another for a distant view. However, a photographer must decide to change a lens. Your eye muscles change the lens's shape automatically.

The light rays inside the camera focus on a chemical layer on film. The points of light change the chemical, forming a pattern. Then the film goes through the developing process. The patterns of light and darkness turn into a photograph.

Inside the eye, the light also forms a pattern on a light-sensitive layer. This layer, at the back of the eye, is called the retina (RET-in-uh). The cells of the retina respond to light. In contrast to a camera with film, the eye processes its images instantly. The cells of the retina send electrical impulses speeding along the optic nerve. When the impulses reach the brain, it makes sense of the image.

The images on film and on the retina are not the same as in real life. Because of the way light rays travel, the image is upside down. To look at a photograph, you must turn it right-side up. To look at the words on this page, however, you don't have to turn the book. Your brain turns the visual image around for you.

A fine camera can be a marvel of engineering. Even the best camera, though, is nowhere near as spectacularly complex as the eye-brain connections you are using right now.

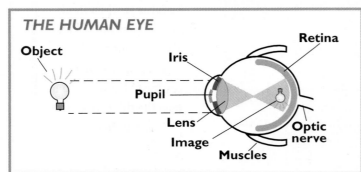

THE HUMAN EYE

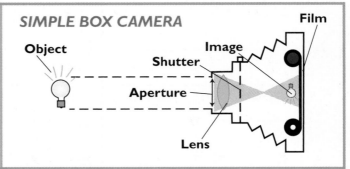

SIMPLE BOX CAMERA

Checking Comprehension

1. Why do you think the brain is so important in the way the eye sees?

    _____

    _____

2. What is the purpose of a lens, and why does it need to change shape?

    _____

    _____

Practicing Comprehension Skills

Write the answer to each question on the lines.

3. Why does a camera need a shutter when an eye does not? What clue word or words signal this difference?

    _____

    _____

4. How is the retina of the eye like the film in a camera? What clue word signals this similarity?

    _____

5. Which can process an image more quickly: the eye or a camera? Explain your answer.

    _____

    _____

6. Fill in the circle before the correct answer.

    Why can people see right-side up?

    ○   Unlike a camera, the eye has no shutter.

    ○   Like a lens, light rays are focused.

    ○   Unlike a camera and photograph, the brain turns upside-down images around for us.

    ○   Like a camera, light enters the eye through a small hole.

Use the Venn diagram below to compare and contrast the eye and the camera.

The Eye   **Both**   **Camera**

7. _____   9. _____   11. _____

_____   _____   _____

8. _____   10. _____   12. _____

_____   _____   _____

Practicing Vocabulary

Write a word from the box to match each definition.

aperture	focus	perspective	pupil	retina	spectacularly	visual

13. _____   hole in a camera that changes size to let in light

14. _____   point of view in judging what you see

15. _____   small hole in eye through which light enters

16. _____   layer of light-sensitive cells at the back of the eye

17. _____   to cause light rays to meet in order to make an image clear

18. _____   having to do with sight

19. _____   in an amazing way

Writing a Compare and Contrast Essay
How is the heart like a pump? How is the brain like a computer? On another sheet of paper, write one or two paragraphs to answer either of those questions or a similar question you make up. Use clue words such as *like*, *also*, *different from*, and *but* to make your comparisons and contrasts clearer.

Summarizing

Writing a summary can help you when you do research or study for a test. A **summary** is a short statement that tells the main ideas and most important details of an article or the main events in a story. These are the same main ideas and important details you would include in notes or in an outline, but they are written in paragraph form. Before you summarize a selection, read it carefully. Look for topic sentences to help you determine the main idea or ideas. Since a summary should be brief, you must choose only the most important information from the events, details, or examples you are given.

The more important information there is in a selection, the longer your summary will be. The summary of a TV show may be two or three sentences. The summary of a book or chapter in a social studies book may be several paragraphs long.

Read the following press release announcing a new TV show. Underline the most important ideas. One paragraph has been done for you. On the lines below, finish writing a summary of the piece that uses only 2-3 sentences.

PRESS RELEASE:

DR. NERO, SUPERHERO

MCP-TV Broadcasting proudly announces a new action-adventure show called "Dr. Nero, Superhero," which will air every Sunday from 9:00 to 9:30 P.M.

Who is Dr. Nero? She's the most thrilling action character ever! A former principal, Dr. Nero gained X-ray vision and the ability to fly after she was accidentally exposed to radioactive isotopes in the school lab. She decided to become . . . Dr. Nero, Superhero! Each Sunday at 9:00 P.M., Dr. Nero helps a student in need to overcome problems ranging from a lost library book to a missed football practice. Watch "Dr. Nero, Superhero," the hottest new show around!

Summary:

MCP-TV is announcing a new action-adventure show called "Dr. Nero, Superhero," which will air on Sundays from 9:00 – 9:30 P.M. _____

_____

_____

Read the following selection. As you read, underline main ideas that you would include in a summary of the selection. The main ideas in the first paragraph have been underlined for you.

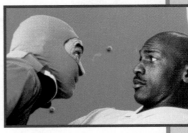

A camera crew wants to shoot a scene in which an actor talks to a cartoon character against an animated background. How can this be done? Many film makers would use the "blue screen" or "green screen" technique. With this process, a character can be shown against any background.

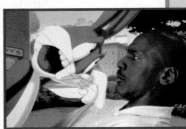

The star would first be filmed in front of a solid blue or green screen. An actor clothed in blue or green might play the cartoon character's part. Cameras would shoot this scene. Then a special computer system would filter the blue or green out of the film. It would be replaced with animation footage.

This technique has many uses in feature films and television shows. It is also used in television weather forecasting, where the weather map replaces the blue or green screen.

Which sentence presents a main idea from the passage that *should* be included in a summary?

○ A camera crew wants to shoot a scene with an actor and a cartoon character.

○ An actor clothed in blue or green might play the cartoon character's part.

○ With this process, a character can be shown against any background.

○ The weather map replaces the blue or green screen.

Which of the following sentences gives the best summary of the third paragraph from the passage?

○ The technique has many uses in movies and television.

○ TV weather forecasting also uses the blue or green screen technique.

○ You have probably seen this technique before.

○ The screen can be blue or green.

On the lines below, write a summary using only three or four sentences. Include the main ideas you underlined.

_____

_____

_____

_____

Tip

A summary tells the most important ideas in as few words as possible. Summarizing helps you to understand, remember, and review information you read or hear.

Read the following article. As you read, think about the main ideas you would include in a summary.

It Lives!

How do filmmakers bring an imaginary creature, such as a dragon or sea monster, to life? How do they turn an ape into a movie star? They use "special effects," techniques referred to as *SFX*.

In the 1930s, a special effects pioneer, Willis O'Brien, made film history with the movie *King Kong*. O'Brien studied the movements of gorillas in zoos to develop small skeletons of a giant ape. He designed eighteen-inch frames and padded them with foam rubber and cotton. Then he covered them with rabbit fur. O'Brien filmed the model using a stop-action camera, which would take one picture, or frame, at a time. He would position the model, take a picture with the camera, then move the model slightly and take another picture. It took hundreds of shots to make the model move for thirty seconds on the screen!

Three large models were used. One was a giant gorilla arm and hand used to hold a frightened actress. Another was a gorilla foot that could descend upon the streets of New York. Finally there was a life-sized model of King Kong built of wood, wire, cloth, and metal. It was covered with bearskins. Three levers controlled Kong's facial movements. King Kong may not look very

realistic to audiences today, but the film terrified people in 1933.

One SFX method is "animatronics," the art of bringing creatures to life by using electronics and remote control. In the 1997 movie *Buddy*, animatronics put another gorilla in a starring role. Artists used puppets and special gadgets to build life-sized models of a gorilla in four stages of life. They also built a gorilla head for a human actor to wear. They punched in each hair by hand. The fake skin and teeth made the head look very realistic. Buddy's movements were what made the special effects so special.

Inside Buddy were control systems made of rods and cables. These were run by a computer to create Buddy's arm, leg, and facial movements. Eyebrows could twitch to show emotion. An air tube would puff to inflate and deflate Buddy's cheeks so that the gorilla seemed to breathe. Buddy's movements were far more realistic than King Kong's. Most people in the audience accepted Buddy as a real gorilla.

Thanks to models and technology, animals can appear on screen today with no need for animal handlers or retakes and with no risk of injuring the animal. Aliens, dinosaurs, and monsters can co-star with humans—and each other! When an audience accepts a creature as real, whether it's terrifying or comical, SFX have done their job.

Checking Comprehension

1. How were the special effects in *King Kong* similar to those in the movie *Buddy*? How were they different?

_____

_____

_____

_____

2. Why do you think filmmakers would rather use animatronic models than real animals?

_____

_____

_____

_____

Practicing Comprehension Skills

Write one sentence to summarize each set of details from the article.
An example is completed for you.

3. Willis O'Brien made film history with the movie *King Kong*.
   O'Brien studied the movements of gorillas in zoos to develop the models he used.
   O'Brien filmed the models using the technique of a stop-action camera.

   Summary: Willis O'Brien made film history with *King Kong* by using special models

   and a stop-action camera.

4. O'Brien used three large models: a giant gorilla arm and hand, a gorilla foot, and a life-sized model.
   Three levers controlled Kong's facial movements.
   The film terrified people in 1933.

   Summary: _____

   _____

5. One SFX method is "animatronics," the art of bringing creatures to life
   by using electronics and remote control.
   In the 1997 movie *Buddy*, animatronics put another gorilla in a starring role.
   Artists used puppets and gadgets to build life-sized models of a gorilla.

   Summary: _____

   _____

6. Artists built a gorilla head for a human actor to wear in the film *Buddy*.
   The artists punched in each hair of the gorilla head by hand.
   Facial features, such as fake skin and teeth, made the head look very realistic.

   Summary: _____

   _____

7. Inside Buddy were control systems made of rods and cables.
   The control systems were run by a computer to create Buddy's arm, leg, and facial movements.
   Buddy's movements were far more realistic than King Kong's.

   Summary: _____

   _____

Read the following statements. Write **Yes** next to each idea that should be included in a
summary of "It Lives!" Write **No** next to ideas that would not be included in a summary.

8. _____ The letters SFX are an abbreviation for "special effects."

9. _____ The art of animatronics uses electronics and remote control.

10. _____ The small model in King Kong was covered with rabbit fur.

11. _____ In the 1930s, Willis O'Brien made film history with *King Kong*.

12. _____ O'Brien used a stop-action camera to bring King Kong to life.

13. _____ The actress in *King Kong* was frightened.

14. _____ The 1997 movie *Buddy* used animatronics to make a gorilla's
    movements seem realistic.

15. _____ Buddy's eyebrows could twitch to show emotion.

16. Review the article "It Lives!" Are all the main ideas from the article listed in items 8-15? Explain your answer.

_____

_____

17. Write a summary of the passage "It Lives!" Be sure you include only the most important information.

_____

_____

_____

_____

Practicing Vocabulary

Write the word from the box that matches each clue.

comical	deflate	descend	electronics	facial	gadgets	remote

18. _____ let the air out

19. _____ has to do with the face

20. _____ move downward

21. _____ humorous

22. _____ small devices

23. _____ distant

24. _____ a science that deals with technology

MAKING THE Reading AND Writing CONNECTION

Writing a Movie Review
Think about a movie you have seen recently. On another sheet of paper, write the title of the movie, a summary of the plot, and whether or not you would recommend that others see it. Be sure to include only the most important information in your summary.

Paraphrasing

Paraphrasing is useful when you take notes in class, study for a test, or research a topic for a report. To **paraphrase** means to restate or explain something in your own words. It is not the same as summarizing. When you summarize, you state the most important points of a piece of writing. When you paraphrase, you restate all the information—not just the important points. A paraphrase should be simpler to read than the original piece.

Read the following article. As you read, think how you could paraphrase the information.

The word *volcano* comes from a story the ancient Romans told about Vulcan, their god of metalworking and fire. They said that Vulcan's workshop was underneath a "fire-breathing" mountain off the coast of Italy. In honor of this god, they gave the name "Vulcano" to the island. Since then, all such mountains have come to be called volcanoes.

Today, we know that a volcano is an opening in the earth's crust. Through this opening, melted red-hot rock is pushed out, often violently. The pressure that pushes the molten rock out is caused by movement of huge slabs of rock that form Earth's shell. As these plates collide, they create friction and pressure that open holes in the crust.

Decide whether the following is a paraphrase or a summary of the first paragraph of the article. On the line, write "paraphrase" or "summary" and explain your choice.

Volcanoes are named for Vulcan, the Roman god of metalworking and fire. Today, all "fire-breathing" mountains are called volcanoes.

_____

Paraphrase the second paragraph.

_____

_____

_____

_____

Tip

When you paraphrase, you can use synonyms for words in the original piece, change word order in sentences, rearrange phrases and clauses, and combine sentences.

As you read the following passage about Mount St. Helens, think about how you would paraphrase the information.

A Mountain Awakes

To some Native people of the Pacific Northwest, the peak was known as "Smoking Mountain." The name Mount St. Helens was given to the mountain in 1792. People thought of it as a serene location for hiking, camping, and other outdoor pleasures. The volcano had been active in the mid-1800s, but its last eruption was in 1857. It had been quiet for over a century.

In March 1980, a number of small earthquakes signaled that the mountain was waking up. On March 20, a "minor" earthquake (4.2 on the Richter scale) occurred. People who lived near Mount St. Helens could feel some of the quakes. Hundreds of small earthquakes followed. Then, on March 27, there was an overwhelming explosion. Ash and steam catapulted 6,000 feet into the air.

Soon an odd bulge developed on one side of the mountain. That bulge was caused by steam and superheated rock gushing from inside the earth. Many people began to feel uneasy.

On May 18, 1980, David A. Johnston, a scientist, was stationed on a post six miles from the volcano. He had just taken some measurements. Two geologists, Keith and Dorothy Stoffel, were flying over the mountain's crater in a small plane. At 8:32 in the morning, an earthquake with a magnitude of 5.1 on the Richter scale loosened the bulge.

"Within a matter of seconds," the Stoffels recall, "the whole north side of the crater began to move instantaneously." Tons of rock and ice began sliding down the mountain in the biggest landslide in recorded history. The earthquake triggered a violent sideways blast of gas, steam, and earth. The blast of superheated material swept across the land at speeds of up to 670 miles per hour, while a cloud of ash shot twelve miles into the air. The pilot of the Stoffels' plane was able to escape the deadly blast, but 57 other people, including David Johnston, were not as lucky.

In addition to the 57 dead, more than 200 homes were leveled by the blast as it raced over the landscape. Thousands of acres of forest were destroyed. Camping grounds, bridges, trails, and miles of highways and railway lines disappeared. About 7,000 large animals died. The birds and smaller animals in the blast area perished.

On May 18, 1983, a ceremony declared the mountain and surrounding land to be the "Mount St. Helens National Volcanic Monument." Since that time, visitors, animals, and plant life have returned, but never again will people take "Smoking Mountain" for granted. Scientists at an observatory named for David Johnston now watch the volcano to help prevent another disaster.

Checking Comprehension

1. Why is it that before the spring of 1980, Washington residents were not concerned about a Mount St. Helens eruption?

   _____

   _____

2. What final events caused the devastation and destruction that occurred on May 18, 1980?

   _____

   _____

Practicing Comprehension Skills

Which of the following is the best paraphrase of these sentences?
Fill in the circle next to the correct answer.

3. Soon an odd bulge developed on one side of the mountain. That bulge was caused by steam and superheated rock gushing from inside the earth. Many people began to feel uneasy.

   ○ The bulge on the mountain's side was odd.

   ○ A strange swelling grew out of one side of the mountain. The swelling, which was created by steam and very hot rock, made many people nervous.

   ○ Many people wondered what was causing the side of the mountain to bulge out.

   ○ Steam and superheated rock could explode at any time. People now thought that the mountain was very dangerous.

4. On May 18, 1980, David A. Johnston, a scientist, was stationed on a post six miles from the volcano. He had just taken some measurements. Two geologists, Keith and Dorothy Stoffel, were flying over the mountain's crater in a small plane.

   ○ The events of May 18, 1980 interested all the scientists in the area.

   ○ Two geologists as well as scientist David A. Johnston were near the volcano on May 18, 1980. All these people were aware that they would be in great danger if an earthquake occurred.

   ○ On May 18, 1980, the safest place to be was an airplane.

   ○ Scientist David A. Johnston was measuring the volcano's activity on May 18, 1980, from a post six miles away. Geologists Keith and Dorothy Stoffel were flying above the crater.

5. Read this paraphrase of the second paragraph of "A Mountain Awakes."
Tell why it is or is not a good paraphrase.

In early spring, 1980, a number of small earthquakes signaled a change.
On March 20 a "minor" earthquake occurred.

_____

_____

6. Write a paraphrase of the last paragraph.

_____

_____

_____

_____

Practicing Vocabulary

Write the word from the box that belongs with each group.

7. red-hot, melting, _____

8. thrown, hurled, _____

9. destroyed, demolished, _____

10. right away, now, _____

11. strength, enormity, _____

12. quiet, peaceful, _____

13. awesome, breathtaking, _____

> catapulted
> instantaneously
> leveled
> magnitude
> overwhelming
> serene
> superheated

Writing a Descriptive Paragraph
Write a short paragraph describing a time you were a witness to an "act of nature," such as a thunderstorm, blizzard, or tornado. Pay close attention to your description of what happened. Then exchange papers with a classmate and paraphrase each other's descriptions.

Recognizing Author's Purpose

When authors write, they usually have a purpose in mind. Four common reasons for writing are:

- To **persuade**: to convince readers to think or act a certain way
- To **inform**: to explain something or give information or directions
- To **entertain**: to amuse or scare readers, or make them feel sadness or joy
- To **express**: to create a mood or feeling through description, to help readers visualize a scene

Sometimes an author has more than one purpose for writing. If you can identify the author's purposes, you will better understand what you read. Knowing the author's purposes can also influence the way you read. When you read a selection that is meant to inform, such as a textbook chapter, you may need to read slowly and carefully. When you read a selection that is meant to entertain, you might want to read more quickly. The author's language and style of writing can help you determine his or her reasons for writing.

Read the following article. Think about the author's purposes for writing.

In Alaska, a dogsled race of over 1,100 miles known as the Iditarod is held annually. Many people wonder how the dogs that participate in this grueling event are trained.

Sled dogs usually begin their training as puppies at around three months of age. They begin by running behind a team of dogs. Some common commands that sled dogs have to learn are *hike* (which means to go) and *easy* (which means to slow down). They also practice pulling light weights with a harness, learning to keep the tug line tight. Trainers quickly weed out dogs that are not intelligent enough or that lack self-control.

Fill in the circle next to the correct answer.

What purpose or purposes do you think the author had for writing this article?

○ to persuade   ○ to entertain   ○ to express   ○ to inform

Think about the way you read this passage. Which of the following selections would you be likely to read in a similar way?

○ a mystery story   ○ a book of jokes   ○ a news article   ○ a poem about dogs

Read the following passage. Think about the author's purposes for writing.

It was my first Iditarod. I didn't expect to win, but I did want to complete the race. Not every musher makes it to the finish line. I wanted that bronze belt buckle stamped with the indelible words, "Iditarod Finisher." I wanted to get my personal police escort down Nome's Main Street to the sound of cheering crowds. Most of all, I wanted to finish for my dogs. I'd been warned about winds that blew snow into solid sheets of blinding whiteness. I'd heard about the moose that blocked your trail like big, shaggy mountains. Yet I knew I had to brave it all for the sake of my beautiful, hard-working team of champions.

What purpose or purposes do you think the author had for writing this article? Explain your answer.

_____

_____

_____

_____

Fill in the circle next to the correct answer or answers.

Which of the following selections would you be likely to read in the same way?

○ a first-person article by an athlete   ○ a chapter in a history book

○ a novel about a dog   ○ a poem

Which of these phrases did the author use to express—to evoke a mood and help you visualize a scene?

○ winds that blew snow into solid sheets of blinding whiteness

○ I did want to complete the race

○ moose that blocked your trail like big, shaggy mountains

○ I didn't expect to win

Tip

As you read, think about the author's reasons for writing the selection. Often the words the author chooses and the style of writing will help you determine the author's purpose.

Jack London's
The Call of the Wild

Jack London

Jack London's *The Call of the Wild* delivers all the thrills and adventure you could possibly want in a book. In this classic novel, you'll follow the journey of Buck, a proud dog whose power, intelligence, and courage make him a hero. Buck's adventure begins as a greedy gardener steals him from a comfortable California home. Buck has never known anything but love and easy living. Now he is beaten and starved, and his new life confounds him. Buck soon finds himself in the brutal setting of the 1897 Alaska gold rush. There, uncaring masters with gold fever put him to work as a sled dog.

The great dog uses every instinct to survive. Buck learns to sleep in snow. Rather than cowering, he fights to be top dog. He wins the respect of every person and beast he meets. Each test Buck faces brings out the best in him.

The Call of the Wild is clearly Buck's story. The only human character London allows the reader to know is John Thornton. Through Buck's eyes, you see Thornton's respect for his dogs and his fitness for life in the wild Yukon. You see love grow as Buck grasps Thornton's hand in his teeth and Thornton playfully shakes the dog's head. However, John Thornton never engages the reader's emotions the way Buck does. It is Buck for whom most readers fear as ice cracks during a river crossing. It is Buck we follow to the very end of the journey.

London clearly describes the sights, sounds, and smells of the frozen North: "Over the whiteness and silence brooded a ghostly calm. There was not the faintest whisper of air—nothing moved, not a leaf quivered, the visible breath of the dogs rising slowly and lingering in the frosty air."

If you've ever loved an animal, *The Call of the Wild* will be a special joy for you. Jack London captures the bond between a human and a dog as no other author has. Yet London insists that every dog is, first, an animal. He reminds us that every animal hears the call of the wild and longs to answer. You will never again look at your family pet in quite the same way after you have read the book.

The Call of the Wild was published in 1903 and has never been out of print. With its gripping scenes and the portrait of an unforgettable dog, the book will keep you on the edge of your seat right up to the last page.

Checking Comprehension

1. Write a sentence that summarizes the author's attitude toward *The Call of the Wild*.

   _____

   _____

2. Based on this review, tell whether or not you would want to read *The Call of the Wild*. Include one or more details to support your point of view.

   _____

   _____

   _____

Practicing Comprehension Skills

3. Fill in the blanks in the chart below. In the blank line on the left, write a purpose that could be described with the sentence provided. In the blank lines on the right, write a sentence that could show the purpose "to inform."

Author's Purpose	Sentence That Shows the Purpose
a. _____	Jack London's *The Call of the Wild* delivers all the thrills and adventure you could possibly want in a book.
b. to inform	_____ _____ _____

4. In your opinion, does the author of this review succeed in meeting the purposes listed above? In two sentences, tell why or why not.

   _____

   _____

Read this passage from *The Call of the Wild* describing a scene in which Buck rescues Thornton from the rapids. Think about author Jack London's purposes for writing.

Buck had sprung in on the instant; and at the end of three hundred yards, amid a mad swirl of water, he overhauled Thornton. When he felt him grasp his tail, Buck headed for the bank, swimming with all his splendid strength. But the progress shoreward was slow; the progress downstream amazingly rapid. From below came the fatal roaring where the wild current went wilder and was rent in shreds and spray by the rocks which thrust through like the teeth of an enormous comb. The suck of the water as it took the beginning of the last steep pitch was frightful, and Thornton knew that the shore was impossible. He scraped furiously over a rock, bruised across a second, and struck a third with crushing force. He clutched its slippery top with both hands, releasing Buck, and above the roar of the churning water shouted: "Go, Buck! Go!"

5. Based on the author's language and style, what do you think his purpose or purposes might have been in writing this scene? Explain your answer.

_____

_____

_____

6. On the lines below, write the author's purpose or purposes that you identified for the passage. Then give a sentence or phrase from the passage that shows the purpose.

Author's purpose: _____

_____

Author's purpose: _____

_____

7. In your opinion, did the author succeed in meeting the purpose or purposes you listed above? In two sentences, tell why or why not.

_____

_____

_____

8. Which of the following selections would you be likely to read in the same way as the passage from *The Call of the Wild*?

○ a chapter in a social studies book ○ an exciting adventure story

○ a poem about a river ○ a newspaper article

Practicing Vocabulary

Choose the word from the box that best replaces the underlined word or words. Write the word on the line to the left.

brooded	brutal	captures	classic	confounds	cowering	instinct

9. _____ Buck's <u>natural behavior</u> often warned him when danger was near.

10. _____ *The Call of the Wild* <u>catches</u> the emotions of the canine hero.

11. _____ The book, like the movie version, is a <u>timeless work</u> that people have enjoyed for generations.

12. _____ Buck never <u>dwelled gloomily</u> over the difficulties of his new life.

13. _____ Rather than <u>hanging back in fear</u>, the brave dog led others forward.

14. _____ The book tells of dogs and humans facing danger in the <u>harsh</u> climate of Alaska and northern Canada.

15. _____ A sudden attack by the other dogs <u>puzzles</u> Buck.

MAKING THE Reading AND Writing CONNECTION

Writing an Eyewitness Account

Think about a memorable animal you have known or one you saw in a zoo or park. What do you know about the animal? How did the animal affect you? Determine a purpose or purposes for writing about this animal: to persuade, inform, entertain, or express. Then write an eyewitness account of your experience with the animal. Be sure to think about your purpose or purposes as you write. Write your paragraph on another sheet of paper.

Statements of Fact and Opinion

When you read, you will often come across statements of fact and statements of opinion.
There are important differences between these types of statements.

A statement of fact can be checked and proved true or false. Even if it is false, it is still considered a statement of fact.

- Tony Meola holds the U.S. National team record for appearances by a goalkeeper.

You can check whether the statement is true or false by looking up the information or by verifying it yourself.

A statement of opinion presents ideas and feelings. It cannot be checked, but it can be supported. Words that signal statements of opinion include *I believe* and *seems to.*

- Tony Meola is one of the best soccer players in the world today.

Valid opinion: Supported by facts or opinions of experts in the field.

Faulty opinion: Either not supported, or supported only by opinions of nonexperts.

As you read the following editorial letter, try to distinguish statements of fact from statements that present the writer's opinions.

Dear Editor,

    I like your soccer articles, but I am unhappy about one thing. Your paper never seems to give any attention to goalkeepers. Please print some articles that feature goalkeepers such as Tony Meola.

    Tony Meola holds the U.S. National team record for most appearances by a goalkeeper. He played in the Major League Soccer All-Star game three years in a row. I believe Meola is one of the best players in soccer today. Just look at the records he set for saves and shutouts.

Write one sentence from the letter that is a statement of fact.
Then name a source you might use to check the fact.

_____

_____

Tip

Write one sentence from the letter that is a statement of opinion. Then tell if the opinion is supported with details.

_____

_____

_____

As you read, pay attention to words or phrases that signal statements of opinion such as *I believe, seems to,* or *in my opinion.*

STRATEGY: Recognizing Statements of Fact and Opinion

Read a sports announcer's comments during the last minutes of the 1999 Women's World Cup final soccer match. As you read, identify statements of fact and statements of opinion.

WORLD CUP 99
THE FINAL GAME

Welcome back, soccer fans! We rejoin the 1999 World Cup final between women of the United States and China. More than 90,000 spectators have gathered at the Pasadena, California, Rose Bowl. It is the largest stadium crowd ever to see a women's sporting event.

We've got a scorching day here in Pasadena. The temperature on the field is more than 100 degrees! Michelle Akers has already fallen victim to the heat. The U.S. defender collapsed after ninety minutes of play. What a loss for team U.S.A.! I believe the U.S. would have scored had Akers remained on the field.

Let me recap the action. After 120 minutes of play, the U.S. and China are tied 0–0. Penalty kicks will settle this game. Each team will have five kick attempts.

China prepares to make its first attempt. Team captain Sun Wen looks nervous.

China's first kick finds the net! Four attempts to go . . . and number two is good! Now midfielder Liu Ying steps to the twelve-yard mark. I don't think she really wants to kick this one! Her shoulders are slumping. She appears tired. U.S. goalkeeper Briana Scurry seems to pick up on Liu Ying's discomfort. Scurry's scowl tells me she's ready for action.

Liu Ying kicks! Briana Scurry dives to her left! She blocks the kick! What a play! China's third attempt has failed! This may well be the turning point of the game! Go, U.S.A.!

China prepares for a fourth penalty kick. The kick is good. Here comes number five. It's in the net.

Four of China's five shots have hit home. That leaves room for the U.S. to win. If there was ever a team to do it, it is this group of warriors. In my mind, they're number one!

The U.S. lines up to kick. A superstitious Briana Scurry impulsively turns her back as her teammate takes the first shot. "I can't look," Scurry's motion seems to say. Yes! The first kick is good! The fans go wild! Surely you listeners can hear them.

Kicks number two, three, four—they are all good! The shoot-out is tied at China 4, U.S. 4. This moment will go down in history!

Now Brandi Chastain is at the mark. The thirty-year-old defender looks composed. The woman has nerves of steel! Chastain's kick propels the ball into the net! She has dropped to her knees. Her teammates are crowding around her. Today Brandi Chastain is America's hero! This must be the greatest moment of her life!

The U.S. women's soccer team has won the World Cup! Remember this moment, sports fans! In my opinion, this victory will change women's athletics forever.

Checking Comprehension

1. Why was the U.S. Women's team able to win the 1999 Women's World Cup?

   _____

   _____

2. Which team do you think the sports announcer favored? What makes you think so?

   _____

   _____

Practicing Comprehension Skills

Find three statements of fact and three statements of opinion in "World Cup 99: The Final Game." Write them below.

Statements of fact:

3. _____

4. _____

5. _____

Statements of opinion:

6. _____

7. _____

8. _____

Find at least five clue words or phrases in the passage that point to a statement of opinion. Write the clue words or phrases on the lines.

9. _____

   _____

10. The following statements were made in the announcer's post-game commentary. On the line before each statement, write **F** if it is a statement of fact and **O** if it is a statement of opinion.

_____ In the first overtime, midfielder Kristine Lilly contributed to the Americans' victory by blocking a headed ball from reaching the goal.

_____ Surely those penalty kicks offered some of the most exciting minutes in sports this year.

_____ Remember, the 1994 Men's World Cup final was also decided on penalty kicks.

_____ Never again will a women's soccer team be as popular as this one!

Practicing Vocabulary

Write a word from the box to match each definition.

attempts	composed	defender	impulsively	propels	recap	superstitious

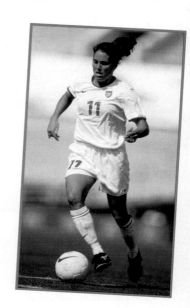

11. _____ a summary of highlights

12. _____ driven by a sudden decision

13. _____ tries

14. _____ one who plays a defensive position

15. _____ calm

16. _____ pushes or drives something forward

17. _____ influenced by fearful beliefs

Writing a Persuasive Paragraph
On another sheet of paper write a paragraph persuading readers that one of your favorite sports teams or stars is the best. Include three statements of fact that could convince your readers. Reread the completed paragraph and underline any statements of opinion.

LESSON 13

Making Judgments

When you read, you make **judgments**, or form opinions, about the people, events, and ideas in the text. To make a judgment, think about your own experiences, the information presented in the text, and the author's purposes for writing.

As you make a judgment, ask yourself, "What made me think this way?" Look for facts that support your opinions. A **valid judgment**, or judgment that is sound, must be based on details in the text. An **invalid judgment** is one that has no support in the text.

As you read the following passage about the *Titanic*, think about judgments you can make about the writer's ideas.

The *Titanic* was called the safest ship ever built. Many said it was "unsinkable." The world's largest ocean liner had the newest safety features. They included a double-layered steel bottom. The hull had sixteen watertight compartments.

The ship also had a wireless radio and a crow's nest with two lookouts. On April 14, 1912, during the ship's first voyage, the lookouts spotted a huge iceberg. They alerted the ship's officers, but it was too late. The iceberg damaged the hull and filled five compartments with water. In the early hours of April 15, the "unsinkable" *Titanic* sank.

Tip

Stop to make judgments as you read. Do not wait until you finish the selection. Question your own judgments as you make them and look for proof in the text.

Which of the following statements is a valid judgment you might make after reading the article? Fill in the circle next to the correct answer.

○ The newest safety features made the *Titanic* unsinkable.

○ The crow's nest lookouts were not doing their job.

○ The newest safety features could not prevent the *Titanic*'s disaster.

○ The *Titanic* was the worst disaster ever.

Which of the following statements is not a valid judgment?
Fill in the circle before the correct answer.

○ The watertight compartments could not keep the *Titanic* afloat.

○ The author believes the *Titanic* was unsinkable.

○ The author believes people were overly confident about the *Titanic*'s safety.

○ The *Titanic* was not "unsinkable."

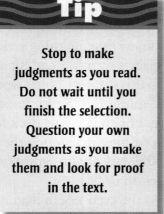

STRATEGY: Making Judgments About Ideas and Text

Read the following article about the last moments in the sinking of the *Titanic*. As you read, make judgments about why so many passengers died.

Abandon Ship!
TO THE LIFEBOATS

In 1912, the *Titanic* sank after striking an iceberg in the North Atlantic. There were about 2,300 people on board. An estimated 1,503 were lost at sea. Did so many people need to die?

At 11:40 P.M. on April 14, passengers felt a jolt. Few knew that anything serious had happened, but the giant steamship had hit an iceberg. For many on board, the next hours would be their last.

Captain E. J. Smith knew that the problem was grave. His crew below deck fought to keep water from rushing in through the damaged hull. At 12:30 P.M., Captain Smith ordered all passengers to gather on deck.

As the crew began loading women and children onto the lifeboats, a frightful truth became clear. If the lifeboats were fully loaded, they would hold only 1,178 passengers. More than 1,000 people had no way to escape the sinking ship! Few could survive in the icy water.

There were more problems. The crew of the "unsinkable" ship had little practice with the new equipment. It took them too long to lower the lifeboats. They also worried that the wooden crafts could not hold much weight. Crew members lowered some of the boats when they were half full.

The passengers, too, were poorly prepared. Many did not understand what was happening. They were slow to board the boats. There had been no emergency drill. Captain Smith, an experienced commander who had sailed for 38 years, seems to have been lax about that vital detail.

Boat after boat left the ship partly filled. There was, by most reports, little panic as women and children said good-bye to the men. Most seemed to expect to be together again soon.

At around 4:00 A.M., the *Carpathia* arrived to rescue the passengers in the lifeboats. On board the rescue ship, many survivors learned the truth. Their husbands and fathers had gone down with the *Titanic*.

Many of the passengers had been famous, wealthy Americans. The public wanted answers. U.S. Senate hearings uncovered outdated safety laws meant for smaller ships. The *Titanic* was 50 percent larger than any other ship afloat. It could carry as many as 3,547 people. Naval laws required it to provide lifeboats for only 1,000. Reports also showed that owners knew there were too few lifeboats on the *Titanic*. It seems that they wanted to keep deck space open for strolling.

Both American and British agencies looked into the sinking. Their findings led to laws that made sea travel safer. In a matter of days, steamship companies were providing enough lifeboats for everyone on board all ships. New rules called for lifeboat drills and crew training. It is unfortunate that it took a tragedy to spur the safety measures.

Checking Comprehension

1. How might the belief that the *Titanic* was "unsinkable" have contributed to the disaster?

_____

_____

_____

2. How did the *Titanic* disaster influence international shipping laws?

_____

_____

Practicing Comprehension Skills

In the first paragraph, the following sentence asks the reader to make a judgment: "Did so many need to die?" Write your judgment about the question on the lines below. Then write three details from the article that support your judgment.

Your Judgment:

3. _____

Supporting details:

4. _____

5. _____

6. _____

7. Read the last sentence of the passage. Does the author draw a valid conclusion based on the evidence in the passage? Give evidence to support your judgment.

_____

_____

_____

8. On the lines before the following judgments, write V if you think the judgment is a valid one. Write I if you think the judgment is invalid.

_____ Safety rules for sea travel were not as strict in 1912 as they are today.

_____ The *Titanic* disaster was all Captain E. J. Smith's fault.

_____ The *Carpathia* could have rescued the survivors more quickly.

_____ Even if the lifeboats had been fully loaded, many passengers would have died.

_____ The public wanted to know why the disaster occurred.

Practicing Vocabulary

Choose a word from the box that best matches each clue.

estimated	hull	lax	lifeboats	steamship	survivors	vital

9. _____ ship operated by steam

10. _____ roughly figured

11. _____ those who live though a catastrophe

12. _____ crafts for saving lives at sea

13. _____ lacking in firmness

14. _____ outer frame of a ship

15. _____ extremely important

Writing a Letter
Think about a family vacation or class field trip you've taken recently. Was it enjoyable? Did it turn out the way you expected it to? What judgments can you make about the experience? Write a letter about your trip, supporting the judgments you make with details. Use another sheet of paper for your letter.

Point of View

What is the difference between these statements?

On Sunday, November 15, 1987, I was born.
Pamela Elizabeth Jones was born on Sunday, November 15, 1987.

Before beginning to write, an author must decide whether the story will be told by one of the characters, as in the first sentence, or by an outsider, as in the second sentence. The perspective from which a story is told is called the **point of view**. An author has several choices for a narrator, or speaker, as the following four versions of the same story show. Each version uses a different point of view. The amount of information given about each character depends on the point of view used.

Version 1

As I climbed the winding staircase, I began to wonder why the thought of reaching the top of the lighthouse had seemed so appealing. Behind me, I could hear my brother Max puffing and his footsteps slowing. Then I arrived at the next window and paused to look out. Gazing open-mouthed at the view below me, I knew why I had made the effort.

Version 2

Growing increasingly short of breath as she climbed the winding lighthouse staircase, Pam couldn't remember why she had wanted to reach the top. When she arrived at the next window, she looked out and thought, "What a gorgeous view! It was certainly worth the effort." Still trudging up the stairs, Max was wondering, "Why did Pam drag me up here, anyway?"

Version 3

Pam had lost count of the stairs as she steadily climbed the winding lighthouse staircase. "Why on earth did I want to reach the top?" she asked herself. Then she reached the next window. Pam gazed out the window and caught her breath. "What a beautiful view!" she told herself. "I'm glad I came after all." She could hear her brother Max's puffing and panting as he trudged up the stairs.

Version 4

Pam climbed the lighthouse stairs steadily, her breath coming more rapidly with each step. When she reached the next window and paused to look out, her eyebrows arched and her mouth dropped. Max was trudging up the stairs behind her.

Answer the following questions about each version of the story by writing **Yes** or **No** on the line in the appropriate column.

	STORY VERSION			
	1	2	3	4
Is the narrator a character in the story?	____	____	____	____
Is the narrator an outsider?	____	____	____	____
Do you know what Pam is doing?	____	____	____	____
Do you know what Pam is thinking?	____	____	____	____
Do you know what Max is doing?	____	____	____	____
Do you know what Max is thinking?	____	____	____	____

First Person Point of View: The narrator is a character in the story. In telling the story from a personal point of view, the "I" narrator, or first person, tells us only her thoughts. She cannot enter the minds of other characters. **Version 1** is told from a first-person point of view.

Third Person Point of View: The narrator is not a character in the story. The narrator uses third-person pronouns such as *he*, *she*, *it*, and *they*. **Version 2, 3, and 4** are told from a third-person point of view. Third-person point of view can be omniscient (all-knowing), limited-omniscient, or dramatic:

Omniscient:
The narrator is an all-knowing outsider who knows the thoughts of all the characters. In the versions of the story, only one gives us both Pam's and Max's thoughts: **Version 2.** This has an **omniscient** point of view.

Limited-omniscient:
A narrator tells the story through the eyes of one character. The narrator is outside the story, but can see into the mind and thinking of one of the characters. **Version 3** has a **limited-omniscient** point of view.

Dramatic:
The narrator describes only what can be seen and heard, like a news reporter. The narrator does not know the thoughts of any of the characters. **Version 4** has a **dramatic** point of view.

Tip

As you read a story, ask yourself, "Who is doing the talking?" Is it an outside observer, or is it someone involved in the story? Whose thoughts does the narrator reveal? The answers to these questions will help you determine the point of view.

The following story is told in four sections, each with a different point of view. As you read, think about how your understanding of the story changes based on the point of view used.

Ben and the Puffins

Section 1

Benjamin Shaw lived with his parents on a light station off Maine's coast. His father, the lighthouse keeper, faithfully climbed the winding lighthouse stairs to illuminate the lantern that warned ships away from the rocky shore. By 1901, when Ben was twelve, some lighthouses had begun the conversion to electric power.

Ben was glad his father's light was still powered by oil. When he helped his father fill the lantern, he thought proudly, "Maybe I'll be the keeper here someday."

Section 2

My favorite time on the island was spring, when the puffins came. I never tired of looking at their colorful, grooved beaks and bright orange feet. I was overjoyed as hundreds of them arrived, returning to the place where they had been born.

Father occasionally viewed the birds with me, though he didn't have much time for bird-watching. First, they would meet at their nesting site from the previous year, for the puffins, while mated for life, were solitary creatures for most of the year.

Section 3

Once the single egg was laid, the parents would take turns incubating it until the little puffling was born. After about two months in the nest, the young pufflings were ready to leave the breeding colony. They would return to the island as adults.

In the spring of 1901, however, only four puffins returned to the island.

"What's wrong, Dad?" Ben asked. "Where are the rest of the puffins?"

"Maybe hunters got them," his father replied. "Some folks eat them, you know. People kill them for their feathers, too."

Section 4

"But that's appalling!" Ben cried.

Ben's father couldn't bear to see his son's disappointment. "Maybe they got caught in a storm," he said quickly.

"Well," Ben replied hotly, "I'm going to protect those four birds. I won't let anyone disturb them while they're nesting. I can—" he paused and thought about what else he could do. "I can make sure no seagulls threaten the pufflings, too!" he said.

"Ben is so much like his grandfather!" thought his father. Aloud, he said, "That's a good plan, son."

Checking Comprehension

1. What are some interesting and unique characteristics of puffins?

   _____

   _____

2. What did Ben enjoy about living on the light station?

   _____

Practicing Comprehension Skills

Fill in the blanks with the correct letter choice:

a. dramatic   **b.** first   **c.** limited-omniscient   **d.** omniscient

3. Third-person _____ point of view tells the reader only what one character is thinking and feeling.

4. Third-person _____ point of view tells the reader what all the characters are thinking and feeling.

5. In _____ person point of view, the narrator is a character in the story.

6. A newspaper reporter would use the third-person _____ point of view.

Answer the following questions about each version of "Ben and the Puffins" by writing **Yes** or **No** on the line in the appropriate column.

	Story Version			
	1	2	3	4
7. Is the narrator a character in the story?	_____	_____	_____	_____
8. Is the narrator an outsider?	_____	_____	_____	_____
9. Do you know what Ben is doing?	_____	_____	_____	_____
10. Do you know what Ben is thinking?	_____	_____	_____	_____
11. Do you know what Ben's father is doing?	_____	_____	_____	_____
12. Do you know what Ben's father is thinking?	_____	_____	_____	_____

Decide if the point of view in each of the sections is:

- • First-person point of view
- • Third-person omniscient point of view
- • Third-person limited-omniscient point of view
- • Third-person dramatic point of view

Write your decision for each section on the line provided, then explain your answer.

13. Section 1: _____

_____

14. Section 2: _____

_____

15. Section 3: _____

_____

16. Section 4: _____

_____

17. Rewrite the following sentences so that they are told entirely from Ben's third-person limited-omniscient point of view.

> I enjoyed everything about living on the light station. I liked the way the waves broke on the rocks and the foghorn's mournful sound. I sometimes thought, "How could I ever live anywhere else?"

_____

_____

_____

18. Rewrite the first paragraph of Section 1 of "Ben and the Puffins," telling the story from a first-person point of view.

_____

_____

_____

_____

19. Which version of the first paragraph of Section I do you prefer: third-person point of view or first-person point of view? Explain your answer.

_____

_____

20. Reread Section 4 of "Ben and the Puffins." How would this section be different if it was retold from a third-person limited-omniscient point of view? What choice would the author have to make about the narrator? Use complete sentences to write your answer.

_____

_____

_____

Practicing Vocabulary

Write a word from the box to complete each sentence.

appalling	conversion	disappointment	illuminate	occasionally	overjoyed	solitary

21. Only _____ could Ben's father join him in bird-watching.

22. The _____ from one power source to another was time-consuming.

23. The idea was so dreadful, Ben found it _____ .

24. Ben was always _____ to watch the unusual birds return to the island.

25. One year, Ben felt terrible _____ when only four birds arrived.

26. The lantern was used as a warning, not to _____ the shore.

27. The company of his parents made Ben's _____ life less lonely.

Writing a Narrative
Use another piece of paper to continue this story of Ben and the puffins. What will happen next? What will Ben do to protect the puffins? Will he be successful? Before you begin, select the point of view from which you will write. You can pretend to be Ben and write from the first-person point of view, or you can write from one of the third-person points of view.

Identifying Text Structure

Text structure refers to the way a piece of writing is organized. Authors choose a particular text structure to fit their purposes and the type of information they are writing about.

There are two main kinds of writing–fiction and nonfiction. **Fiction** stories, which tell of imaginary people and events, are often organized in the time order in which they occur, or chronological order. **Nonfiction** tells of real people and events, or tells information about the real world. Nonfiction writers can use several different ways to organize their work. Following are some of the ways that a piece of writing can be organized:

Chronological Order	This form of text structure organizes a piece of writing by the order in which events occur. Fiction stories and novels are often organized this way. Nonfiction works that use chronological order can include biographies and autobiographies, and articles or books that describe historical events or time periods. Clue words such as **at first, later,** and **eventually,** as well as dates of important events, signal chronological order.
Cause and Effect	Nonfiction pieces can be organized by showing cause-and-effect relationships. Sometimes the causes and effects are directly stated. For instance, a newspaper article reporting that a government official has resigned will go on to state why the official resigned if the causes are known. Other times, either the cause or effect is not stated. Instead, the causes or effects are implied. Look for clue words such as **because, as a result,** and **therefore** to signal causes and effects.
Compare and Contrast	A piece of nonfiction writing that is organized by compare and contrast shows how two subjects are alike, different, or both alike and different. Look for clue words such as **similarly, like, in addition,** or **in the same way** to signal likenesses. Clue words such as **but, however, different, unlike,** or **on the other hand** show differences. The author may directly state the relationship between the two subjects, or the ways in which the subjects are alike and different may be implied.
Main Idea	Nonfiction writers often organize a paragraph, passage, or article by main idea and supporting details. The main idea is the writer's most important idea about the topic. It may be stated in a topic sentence or it may be implied. Supporting details give more information about the main idea.
Problem and Solution	This nonfiction text structure presents both a problem and the solution to the problem. An editorial might be arranged this way, with a problem stated at the beginning and the writer's suggested solution at the end.

Read the following paragraphs. Think about how the text is organized and what effect this has on the information presented.

Paragraph 1

Sarah Chang was born in Philadelphia in 1980. She began to take violin lessons when she was just four years old. She played so well that she was performing with local orchestras by the time she was five. Word of Sarah's talent spread to the conductor of the New York Philharmonic Orchestra. When he heard her play, he invited her to appear as a soloist with his famous orchestra. Sarah was just eight years old. After her momentous performance, the Philharmonic audience was silent. Then, suddenly, the crowd burst into cheers. Since that exciting day, Sarah has recorded several CDs and now appears with orchestras all over the world.

How is this passage organized? Explain your answer.

_____

_____

What might have been the author's purpose in choosing this text structure?

_____

Paragraph 2

I'm so excited! I'm going to play a violin solo at the Metropolitan Concert Hall next week, and I'll get to meet my idol, Sarah Chang! First, I want to ask her how she manages to devote so much time to scales. I've read that, unlike me, she really keeps up her scales. She has also managed to balance her music with her family and study time. I, however, have trouble doing that, and I would like her advice. Finally, I know she gets a lot of support from her parents and brother. My family supports me in the same way. I'd like her to know that we have something in common!

1. How is this passage organized? Explain your answer.

_____

_____

2. Did you use clue words to decide how the passage was organized? Explain your answer.

_____

_____

Tip

As you read a story or article, think about how the text is organized and what that tells you about the author's purpose.

Read the following biography of another famous musician. As you read, think about how the text is structured and how this organization affects the tone of the writing.

Mozart: The Wonderchild

Wolfgang Amadeus Mozart was one of Austria's most famous musicians. What is really interesting is that Mozart became famous at a very early age. When he was only six, he was performing all over Europe. In 1768, when he was twelve, he wrote his first opera. How did Mozart become so successful at such an early age?

The most important factor in Mozart's success was his talent. He was composing music by age five and wrote his first published works, four violin sonatas, at the age of eight. He could make up music at the keyboard, improvise songs to go with melodies composed by others, and play any piece of music in any style—even when blindfolded. His talent made him a great favorite with audiences, who called him the *wunderkind* (VUN-der-kint), a German word meaning *wonderchild*.

Furthermore, Mozart was successful because of the determination of his father. Leopold Mozart wanted young Wolfgang to be a composer, especially since the boy showed such early promise. The Mozarts were a musical family, and the house was always full of the sounds of instruments and singing.

Wolfgang learned to read and play music when he was a small child. His father decided to show him off to audiences when he was very young. He played in the courts and palaces of the major European cities. Although Wolfgang was already a favorite of the emperor of Austria, his father was always urging him to work harder and do better. Only a few musicians at that time became rich, but Leopold thought that his son deserved wealth and fame.

Finally, Wolfgang Mozart was successful because he genuinely loved music. As a child, he enjoyed surprising his father with little tunes he had written. Some were so technically challenging that even longtime professional musicians could not play them! By the time of his early death at age 35, Mozart had composed more than 600 works.

Today, Mozart's music is performed all over the world. There are Mozart festivals in many big cities every summer. Because of Mozart's great talent, the influence of his father, and his love for music, he is considered one of the most brilliant composers who ever lived.

Checking Comprehension

1. What do you think some of Wolfgang Mozart's character traits were when he was young?

   _____

   _____

2. Imagine yourself in Mozart's place. Would you say your childhood was a happy one? Why or why not?

   _____

   _____

   _____

Practicing Comprehension Skills

3. What text structure is used in "Mozart: The Wonderchild"? Why do you think the writer chose this structure?

   _____

   _____

Complete the chart to show the text structure used in "Mozart: The Wonderchild."
Fill in the blank on the left by giving another reason for Mozart's early fame. Fill in the blanks on the right by writing the effects.

Causes	Effects
4. Mozart was talented.	_____ _____
5. _____ _____	He learned to read and play music as a small child. He played for audiences when he was only six.
6. Mozart loved music.	_____ _____

7. What might a chronological approach to Mozart's life have told the reader that this article does not say?

_____

_____

_____

Read the following letter to a newspaper. Think about how the text is organized and what effect this has on the information presented.

We Need an Orchestra Parents Association!

Dear Editor,

Our middle school orchestra is asked to play at events all around the state. Last week, however, we had to turn down an invitation to play because of lack of funds for a bus. It is expensive to transport an entire orchestra, plus instruments, to a distant town. Everyone felt bad about this decision. I have a solution: we need an Orchestra Parents Association. My friend in another town belongs to his school orchestra, and they have an OPA. This group of parents raises funds for the orchestra. They sell snacks at concerts and hold garage sales and raffles to raise money. We have many caring orchestra parents here in the middle school. Let's start our own Orchestra Parents Association!

8. Is this a fiction or nonfiction passage? Explain your answer.

_____

9. Describe the text structure of "We Need an Orchestra Parents Association!" What effect does the text structure have on the information presented?

_____

_____

Read this newspaper article. Think about how the text is organized.

ORCHESTRA PARENTS ASSOCIATION FOUNDED AT READING MIDDLE SCHOOL

The first meeting of the Reading Middle School Orchestra Parents Association will be held on Tuesday, March 21, at 7:30 P.M. at the home of James and Georgia Lewis on 121 Smith Road. All interested parents of students in the middle school orchestra are invited to attend to discuss future fundraising ideas. Mr. and Mrs. Lewis are both cello players with the Metropolitan Orchestra. Their son, James Jr., plays the viola in the middle school orchestra.

10. Is this a fiction or nonfiction passage? Explain your answer.

_____

11. How is the article organized? Explain your answer.

_____

_____

_____

Practicing Vocabulary

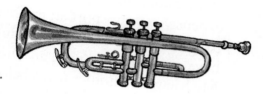

Choose the word from the box that best fits each blank in the paragraph. Write the correct words on the blanks.

| challenging | composers | emperor | improvise | influence | melodies | urging |

One of my piano teacher's favorite _____ is Mozart. Some of Mozart's

_____ are extremely _____ for a young artist to play. I've learned a few

Mozart pieces because my teacher was _____ me to. My teacher says the composer's

work was a strong _____ on her career. However, I really prefer to _____

my own pieces. I'm glad I don't have a royal _____ to please, as Mozart did!

MAKING THE Reading AND Writing CONNECTION

Writing a Paragraph
What are you good at doing? Do you write or draw, or play an instrument or a sport? On a separate sheet of paper, write a paragraph about your talent, using one of the text structures you learned in this lesson.

Understanding Author's Viewpoint

An **author's viewpoint** is the way an author looks at the subject he or she is writing about. Authors can choose to take a viewpoint that is either balanced or biased.

In **balanced writing**, the reader is presented with facts and opinions from more than one viewpoint. Readers are usually left to make up their own minds. This news report shows balanced writing: "The leader of the parents' organization reported on the study of Norwood's school lunches. He said the study showed the lunches were lacking in nutritional value. The president of the Make-a-Lunch Company responded, 'Our school lunches meet every nutritional standard.' "

In **biased writing**, the reader can detect a strong feeling for or against someone or something. The writer will present only one viewpoint or one side of an argument. The use of "loaded" words meant to bring out the reader's emotions is often a clue that biased writing is present. In this news report, the words *totally* and *blustered* indicate biased writing.: "The leader of the parents' organization said the study proved that the nutritional value of the Norwood School lunches was totally inadequate. In response, the Make-a-Lunch Company blustered about standards."

As you read this letter to a school newspaper, consider the author's viewpoint. Is it balanced or biased?

Dear Editor:

Yesterday I read that our Congress is allotting billions more dollars for the space program this year. Aren't there more important things we could do with that money? For example, what about all the schools that lack funding for computers? What about the schools that can't offer special programs, such as art and music? Couldn't some NASA money be spent on funding for these things? It's outrageous to waste money sending people into space when there are far more meaningful ways to spend our money.

Signed,
Mary Lee, Montrose, AZ

Does the writer of this letter have a balanced or biased viewpoint?

_____

What evidence in the letter supports your judgment?

_____

_____

Tip

Biased writing contains loaded words that try to slant a reader's view. Some examples of loaded words are *terrible, wonderful, horrible,* and *sensible.*

Read this speech a sixth-grader gave to a school assembly. Watch for words the speaker uses to express a viewpoint. Judge for yourself if that viewpoint is balanced or biased.

Support Young Astronauts!

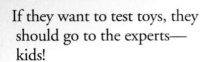

My fellow students, I am very interested in the space shuttle and our country's attempts to explore space. Recently, I read a newspaper article about toys that were taken into space, but they weren't taken for diversions. The astronauts used them for science experiments!

Astronaut John Casper had a ball that was attached to a cup with a string. He tried to get the ball into the cup. This task was much harder than it sounds because in space there is no gravity to pull the ball down.

Astronaut Mario Runco performed some experiments with a toy car and a track. On Earth, he had pushed a toy car around a circular track that stood on its side. The car went around the track until friction slowed the wheels to a stop. Then gravity caused it to fall off the track. In orbit, the car just stopped when the friction of the wheels made it stop. Because there is no gravity in space, the car stayed on the track and didn't fall off.

What is my point? If NASA is going to waste billions of critical dollars on the space shuttle program so people can play with toys in space, then they should send children like us on these missions!

If they want to test toys, they should go to the experts— kids!

There are obvious benefits to letting kids perform these experiments. Kids who are chosen would get fantastic training that they could use in their future. Back on Earth, they could share their enthusiasm. This, in turn, would make other kids support NASA. Remember, kids grow up to become voters! Most important, using kids to perform these experiments would allow the astronauts to spend their time on more crucial matters. NASA could also send two ninety-pound kids for every 180-pound adult.

Do you need more reasons? Think about this. Most kids play on sports teams, so we know about teamwork and playing by the rules. Finally, space travel may well become an everyday event in the near future. Children need to be prepared.

Please, fellow students, talk to your parents and your teachers. E-mail your senators and representatives. We desperately need to stand together on this important issue. Children belong in space!

Checking Comprehension

1. What are some experiments on toys that were performed in space?
   How were they different in space?

   _____

   _____

   _____

2. What would be some benefits of using children as astronauts?

   _____

   _____

Practicing Comprehension Skills

3. What is the author's viewpoint about sending children on space missions?

   _____

4. Is the speech balanced or biased? Why do you think so?

   _____

   _____

5. Give examples of loaded words in the speech.

   _____

6. Fill in the circle next to the sentence that does not express bias.
   Explain your answer on the lines provided.

   ○ NASA is wasting billions of dollars so people can play with toys in space.

   ○ Kids who are chosen would get fantastic training.

   ○ Recently I read a newspaper article about toys that were taken into space.

   ○ Children belong in space!

   _____

   _____

7. Rewrite these sentences so that they present a more balanced viewpoint. Remember to show both sides of the issue, such as whether there could also be benefits in NASA's approach to the toy experiments.

   If NASA is going to waste billions of critical dollars on the space shuttle program so people can play with toys in space, then they should send children like us on these missions! If they want to test toys, they should go to the experts: kids! There are obvious benefits to letting kids perform these experiments.

   _____

   _____

   _____

   _____

Practicing Vocabulary

Write the word from the box that belongs with each group of words.

circular	critical	diversions	enthusiasm	experiments	friction	obvious

8. rubbing, resistance, _____

9. clear, plain, _____

10. round, like a circle, _____

11. tests, trials, _____

12. eagerness, interest, _____

13. amusements, pleasures, _____

14. important, crucial, _____

MAKING THE Reading AND Writing CONNECTION

Writing a Letter to the Editor
On another sheet of paper, write a letter to your local newspaper about an issue you care about. Before writing, decide whether your writing will show a balanced or a biased viewpoint. Be able to explain the language you used to indicate this.

Making Generalizations

A **generalization** is a conclusion that you can make after thinking about a number of examples or facts and what they have in common. Generalizations help you recognize an author's purpose and evaluate possible bias. Clue words that can signal a generalization include *all, none, most, many, always, everyone, never, sometimes, some, usually, seldom, few, generally, in general,* and *overall.*

Generalizations can be valid or faulty. A **valid** generalization is one that is supported by facts or logic. A **faulty** generalization is not completely supported by facts. As you read, look for generalizations the writer makes. Decide whether they are supported by facts.

Read the following paragraphs. As you read, think about generalizations the author makes. Also think about generalizations that you can make.

Crack! Lightning strikes a tree in the middle of the forest. Soon the dry underbrush is aflame. Before the fire can get out of hand, special firefighters are preparing to parachute from a plane. These firefighters, called smokejumpers, are usually in the air within ten minutes of the call.

Once the fire has been located and evaluated, smokejumpers jump to a safe spot nearby. Generally, smokejumpers begin by cutting down nearby sources of fuel for the fire and digging a trail that surrounds the fire. Both of these steps will usually contain the fire. Then the smokejumpers attack the fire itself, cooling it down with dirt and spading the burned area.

Decide whether the following sentence is a generalization. Explain your answer.

These firefighters, called smokejumpers, are usually in the air within ten minutes of the call.

_____

_____

Find a generalization in the second paragraph. Explain how you know it is a generalization.

_____

_____

_____

Tip

Clue words can help you spot generalizations, but some generalizations do not include clue words. If you can mentally add a clue word to a sentence without changing the meaning, then the statement is probably a generalization.

On Your Own What is it like to be a smokejumper—a firefighter who parachutes to the location of wildfires? Veteran smokejumper Arlen Cravens is manager of the Region 5 Smokejumper Base in Redding, California. As you read the following interview with Mr. Cravens, look for generalizations that he makes, as well as generalizations you can make from what he says.

An Interview with Smokejumper ARLEN CRAVENS

Q: Have you always been a smokejumper?
A: I started out as a hot shot. Hot shot crews are twenty-person firefighting teams. They work as a single unit and are called in to fight the largest, most difficult wilderness fires. The smokejumper mission is the initial attack. Our motto is: "Hit 'em hard and keep 'em small."

Q: What made you want to become a smokejumper?
A: When I was in eighth grade, I was failing English. My teacher said that the only way I would pass was if I wrote a three-page paper on what I wanted to be when I grew up. So I went to the school library for ideas. They had a row of about eight or ten file cabinets. I started at A in the first cabinet. When I got to S, I saw something that looked like a deep-sea diver. I thought, "That looks interesting." It turns out that it was a smokejumper from Redding. I was interested!

Q: Were you a parachutist before you became a smokejumper?
A: No, we look for experienced wildland firefighters. We train them to become parachutists.

Q: What's the best part about being a smokejumper?
A: The camaraderie. There is great camaraderie among our crew and among the other 360 American smokejumpers. Smokejumping also provides a sense of accomplishment. Another exciting part is not knowing where you'll end up at the end of a day. We are based in Redding, but by nightfall we may be fighting a fire anywhere from the southern California Sierras to central Oregon.

Q: Are there any women smokejumpers?
A: Nationally, there are more than 30 female smokejumpers.

Q: How do you feel when you get a call?
A: Excited. When you're not working on a fire, you're maintaining the gear or exercising. You never know when the alarm will sound. When it does, you are ready and eager to answer the call.

Q: How long are you typically at a fire?
A: Normally, we're there two days and two nights. A three-day supply of food and water is dropped by parachute when we jump. Smokejumpers fight fires without water, and that takes time. When we leave, we leave with the fire out. We dig up the dirt, then we get down on our hands and knees and feel every inch to make sure it is cool.

Q: What special equipment do you use?
A: We wear fire-resistant jumpsuits with padding. We use chain saws and crosscut saws. We are probably the last experts in the use of the crosscut saw. That's the one with handles at each end for two people to use.

Q: What qualities do smokejumpers need?
A: Smokejumpers need desire, tenacity, and the ability to set a goal and stick to it.

Checking Comprehension

1. How is a smokejumper's work different from that of a regular firefighter?

_____

_____

2. What physical skills would someone probably need to be a smokejumper?

_____

_____

Practicing Comprehension Skills

Fill in the circle next to each answer. Then explain your choice by writing your answer on the lines.

3. Which of the following is a generalization, not a simple fact?

○ a. Normally, smokejumpers are at a fire for two days and two nights.

○ b. The smokejumper mission is the initial attack.

○ c. Hot shot crews are teams of 20 firefighters.

○ d. The smokejumpers in Region 5 cover the territory from the southern Sierras to central Oregon.

4. **Explanation:** _____

_____

5. Which of the following generalizations is <u>valid</u>, based on facts in the interview?

○ a. Any parachutist can become a smokejumper.

○ b. Smokejumpers usually use water to put out fires.

○ c. Smokejumpers always need to be able to work well with others.

○ d. All smokejumpers were on hot shot crews before they became smokejumpers.

6. **Explanation:** _____

_____

7. Which of the following generalizations is <u>faulty</u>, judging from the interview?

    ○ **a.** Smokejumping is often unpredictable work.

    ○ **b.** In general, smokejumping is much like deep-sea diving.

    ○ **c.** Some smokejumpers are women.

    ○ **d.** Smokejumpers are usually busy, even when they are not fighting fires.

8. **Explanation:** _____

_____

9. Complete the following statement with a generalization you can make based on facts from the text or your previous knowledge and experience.

    All smokejumpers need to be _____

_____

Practicing Vocabulary

Choose the word from the box that best fits each blank in the paragraph. Write the correct words on the blanks.

10.   When the request came into the dispatcher's office, the smokejumpers

were _____ their equipment. Quickly they suited up for

their _____ and boarded the plane. There was a friendly

spirit of _____ as they prepared to spend three days

together in the rugged _____ . A _____

is both a firefighter and a trained _____ , and soon the

crew was parachuting from the plane in small groups. They were ready to fight

the fire with great _____ .

camaraderie
maintaining
mission
parachutist
smokejumper
tenacity
wilderness

MAKING THE
Reading
AND
Writing
CONNECTION

Writing an Advertisement
Create a recruiting poster for smokejumpers. Include generalizations about the work and about the kind of person who would find this job exciting and fulfilling. Use a separate sheet of paper for your poster.

Outlining

A good way to understand what you read is to make an **outline**. An outline is a list of information that shows how an author organized the different ideas in a piece of writing. Brief **headings** capture the most important information in an outline. Before you begin making an outline, you need to choose whether you will write all your headings as sentences, as phrases, or as key words.

A good outline shows how the author's main topics, subtopics, and important details are organized. A **main topic** is written next to **Roman numerals I, II, III,** and so on. Main topics are divided into two or more **subtopics**, which give more information about the main topic. Subtopics are written next to **capital letters A, B, C,** and so on. Important **details** give information to support the subtopics. They are written next to **numerals 1, 2, 3,** and so on.

Read the following passage and look at the outline beside it. Fill in the blank spaces with any missing main topics, subtopics, and details.

San Francisco's Cable Cars

On September 1, 1873, several people boarded a cable car in San Francisco. This trip was the first cable car ride in the United States.

Cable cars get their name from the long wire cord or cable that runs beneath the streets of the cars' route. The cable looks like a giant moving clothesline with a pulley at each end. A huge power source turns the pulleys and makes the cable pull the cars up and down the city's steep hills. Each car has a large, powerful claw under its floor. This claw grips the cable when the car is ready to move and lets go when the car needs to stop.

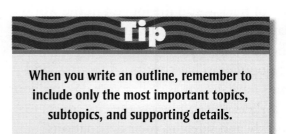

Tip

When you write an outline, remember to include only the most important topics, subtopics, and supporting details.

(Title)	San Francisco's Cable Cars
(Main Topic)	**I.** The first U. S. cable car
(Subtopics)	**A.** Year 1873
	_____
(Main Topic)	_____
(Subtopic)	**A.** Cable below streets
(Details)	_____
	2. Pulleys move cable
(Subtopic)	**B.** How cable cars stop and go
(Details)	_____
	_____
	2. Claw beneath car releases cable to stop

On Your Own

Read the following article about the New York City subway system. As you read, think about the most important information you would include in an outline of this article.

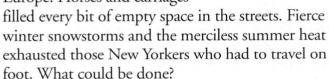

ALL ABOARD! A Trip Through New York's Subways

At the turn of the twentieth century, New York City was a busy place. The city was growing so quickly that new houses and apartment buildings were going up every day. Downtown, the sidewalks were jammed with shoppers, workers, travelers, and newly arrived immigrants from Europe. Horses and carriages filled every bit of empty space in the streets. Fierce winter snowstorms and the merciless summer heat exhausted those New Yorkers who had to travel on foot. What could be done?

An underground railroad, or subway, seemed to be the solution to these problems. Railroads moved on their own tracks, so they never sat in traffic jams. Powered by strong engines, railroads could do the work of many horses. Horses had to be fed and cared for, and they could get sick or go lame. However, if an engine failed, it could be repaired or replaced. Building the railroad under the ground made perfect sense. It would ease congestion on the crowded streets of Manhattan. Most of the city's major business districts were located in this borough, which is on a small and narrow island.

A subway was not a new idea to New Yorkers. The first subway in the world had opened in London back in 1863. However, the question of who would build and own a subway in New York City had never been decided. In 1888, New York's mayor, Abram Hewitt, proposed a law that said the city government should build and own the subway. This idea was finally accepted. Building a subway would be backbreaking work for 12,000 people, but many New Yorkers were eager for steady work, even if it was hard.

In 1904, the mayor of New York City put on his good coat and a top hat and guided the first train north from City Hall in downtown Manhattan to Grand Central Station on 42nd Street. It then ran west to Times Square, the midpoint of the modern city. From Times Square the train went north again up Broadway to 145th Street. The total distance was a little over nine miles, and it took just 26 minutes. That same day, 100,000 excited New Yorkers rode the brand-new train. The fare was just 5¢.

By 1913, the subway was so popular that officials made plans to extend the system. The cost, over $300 million, was sky-high. Up to that time, the only building project that had cost more was the Panama Canal. However, the expansion was worth the money. When it was finished, there were 656 miles of track—still the longest in the world.

Today, the New York City subway remains the most efficient way to get around the city 24 hours a day. The population has continued to grow, and traffic jams have grown as well. Every day, millions of New Yorkers descend below the city streets to travel quickly and safely to their destinations. However, the fare is now much more than a nickel!

Checking Comprehension

1. Why was a subway system needed in New York City?

   _____

   _____

2. What is one of the benefits of the New York City subway system?

   _____

   _____

Practicing Comprehension Skills

3. Complete an outline of the article by filling in the missing topics, subtopics, and details.

   _____

I. Need for a new transportation system

   _____

   _____

II. Benefits of a subway

   _____

   B. Trains stronger and easier to maintain
      than horses

   _____

III. Building the subway

   A. Question of ownership

      _____

      _____

IV. The first New York subway

   A. Year was 1904

   B. Ran from City Hall to Broadway
      and 145th Street

      _____

      _____

   C. 100,000 riders

      _____

      _____

   B. Runs 24 hours a day

      _____

On the line below, list a detail from the article that is not closely related enough to the topic to belong in an outline.

4. _____

5. If the article had an additional paragraph at the end containing a new main topic, how would that topic be indicated on the outline?

_____

6. Fill in the blanks in the paragraph.

Main topics are written next to _____ . Main topics are divided into

two or more _____ , which are written next to _____ .

Important _____ give information to support the _____

and are written next to _____ .

Practicing Vocabulary

Choose the word from the box that best matches each clue. Write the word on the line.

7. _____ antonym for *broke*

8. _____ antonym for *emigrants*

9. _____ synonym for *underground train*

10. _____ antonym for *kind*

11. _____ synonym for *fullness*

12. _____ synonym for *center*

13. _____ antonym for *refreshed*

congestion

exhausted

immigrants

merciless

midpoint

repaired

subway

Writing an Outline

Write a short nonfiction article about a topic that interests you. Use the Internet or an encyclopedia if you need ideas or facts. Be sure to organize your article so that it contains main topics, subtopics, and details. Then trade papers with a partner. On another sheet of paper, make an outline of your partner's article as your partner outlines what you wrote.

Persuasive Devices and Propaganda

If you've ever listened to an advertisement on radio or television, you have probably come across **propaganda**. Propaganda is the spreading of ideas in order to convince people to believe, do, or buy something. You can find propaganda in political speeches and in most advertising. Five **persuasive devices** often used in propaganda are shown in the chart below.

When a writer's purpose is to persuade you, he or she presents evidence to convince you. Some evidence is more valid than others. To become a wise reader, you should look at the evidence the writer offers and decide whether or not you can trust that evidence.

Device	Definition	Example
Testimonial	A testimonial is something a person says to recommend someone or something.	Basketball pro Hoop Hooper says, "I wear Pro-Rite shoes in every game. So should you!"
Bandwagon	This device suggests that many people are buying or doing something, so it must be the right thing to do.	Last year, 40,000 Americans bought Fast-Tek Mountain Bikes. What are you waiting for?
Loaded Words	Loaded words try to slant a reader's view of a product or person. Loaded words have strong connotations that are not necessarily true.	Refreshing, delicious, nutritious — Bright Star Lemonade is one unique drink! Mmmm!
Vague Generalities	Vague generalities are statements that are purposely broad or vague. They give few specific details and offer little evidence to back up their claims.	Moe Mullins is the best candidate for mayor, because Moe gets results!
Sweeping Generalizations	Sweeping generalizations give some sort of "truth" but offer little evidence. They speak for a large group or overstate a situation. They often include such words as *always, never, all, no one, none,* and *everyone*.	At Val's Diner, you'll never be disappointed. Val's always serves the best meals at the lowest prices!

Circle the name of the propaganda device that each statement uses.

Candidate Mary Brown is independent, hardworking, and courageous.

    testimonial   bandwagon   loaded words

Champion dog trainer Rory Rolfe says, "My dogs roll over and beg for Doggie Yum-Yums!"

    testimonial   vague generalities   sweeping generalizations

Read the following radio ad for Petster's Pet Shop. Look for persuasive devices as you read.

Studies show that people with pets are happy people. That's why more and more Americans are becoming pet owners. Perhaps the time is right for you to share your life with a pet. At Petster's Pet Shop, we are ready to help you take that important step.

Stop by our clean, pleasant shop anytime. Get to know our happy family of pets. Talk to our caring pet professionals.

Now, don't just take our word for it. Listen to what Dr. Dan Noto, radio's famous pet vet, had to say: "For pet perfection, go to Petster's!" That's right, Dr. Dan! No one knows more about pets than we do. Our pets always make the best pets. So make Petster's *your* pet center today. You'll never be lonely again!

What persuasive device does this sentence from the ad illustrate? Explain your answer.

"Studies show that people with pets are happy people."

_____

What persuasive device is used in this sentence? How do you know?

"That's why more and more Americans are becoming pet owners."

_____

_____

What persuasive device is mainly used in this paragraph from the ad?

"Stop by our clean, pleasant shop anytime. Get to know our happy family of pets. Talk to our caring pet professionals."

_____

What two persuasive devices are used in paragraph 3 of the ad? How do you know?

_____

_____

_____

If an author's purpose is to convince you to believe, do, or buy something, the writing is propaganda. Once you identify propaganda, think about facts and ideas that the author fails to mention.

Read this script for a television commercial. Think about the propaganda devices as you read.

"World Traveler"

Nutribeef Dog Food Ad

EXTERIOR: HIGH ON A SNOWY MOUNTAINTOP—DAY

A dog sits on the side of a mountain. He sniffs the air, sniffs it again, then runs down the snowy slope.

EXTERIOR: DESERT IN AFRICA

The dog runs across desert sands.

EXTERIOR: EIFFEL TOWER

The dog makes a circuit around the Eiffel Tower in Paris and sniffs again.

EXTERIOR: SHIP IN NEW YORK HARBOR NEAR THE STATUE OF LIBERTY

The dog passes the Statue of Liberty, still sniffing.

EXTERIOR: STREETS OF NEW YORK CITY

The dog runs up and down streets of New York City in pursuit of the delicious aroma. He stops and sniffs. Then he spies a luxurious apartment building and trots toward it. A woman holding a bag of groceries enters the building. The dog follows her inside.

INTERIOR: APARTMENT—DAY

The woman opens her grocery bag and pulls out a can of Nutribeef dog food.

WOMAN (to the dog): "I bet you're hungry, boy."

DOG: "Woof, woof!"

WOMAN: "Here's a bowl of scrumptious and nutritious Nutribeef dog food!"

The woman puts dog food in a bowl. The dog eats hungrily.

VOICE-OVER (Narrator): "Dogs will travel any distance for a delicious bowl of Nutribeef Dog Food. It's right on the label: Nutribeef contains meaty chunks of real beef. What dog doesn't love beef? Dogs know that Nutribeef is the tastiest dog food made. They flock from all over the world to get a bite of Nutribeef, because it's worth it! Nutribeef also has all the nutrition your dog ever needs. More and more dog owners are choosing Nutribeef. Shouldn't you choose it, too?"

Checking Comprehension

1. What point is this commercial trying to make?

   _____

   _____

2. Would you be influenced by this advertisement? Explain why or why not.

   _____

   _____

   _____

Practicing Comprehension Skills

Fill in the circle before the persuasive device used in each sentence. Then on each line, write the words that gave you clues about the device used.

3. Dogs know that Nutribeef is the tastiest dog food made.

   ○ testimonial   ○ vague generality   ○ bandwagon   ○ sweeping generalization

   _____

4. More and more dog owners are choosing Nutribeef.

   ○ testimonial   ○ loaded words   ○ bandwagon   ○ sweeping generalization

   _____

5. Here's a bowl of scrumptious and nutritious Nutribeef Dog Food!

   ○ vague generality   ○ testimonial   ○ loaded words   ○ bandwagon

   _____

6. Nutribeef has all the nutrition your dog ever needs.

   ○ testimonial   ○ loaded words   ○ bandwagon   ○ sweeping generalization

   _____

7. Give an example of a testimonial the television script writer might have included in this advertisement.

_____

_____

_____

8. Think about the name *Nutribeef.* Would you agree that this made-up word is an example of a loaded word? Why or why not?

_____

_____

_____

Suppose you wanted to persuade people to switch dog food brands to Nutribeef. Think of a sweeping generalization and a bandwagon device you might use to persuade them. Write your answers on the lines below.

9. Sweeping Generalization

_____

_____

10. Bandwagon

_____

_____

Rewrite these statements, providing facts that could be used to support them.

11. Nutribeef has all the nutrition your dog ever needs.

_____

_____

12. More and more dog owners are choosing Nutribeef.

_____

_____

13. Look back at the commercial for Nutribeef. Are any of the claims it makes valid, supported by facts or evidence? Explain your answer.

_____

_____

14. Circle the dog food names below that use loaded words.

Yummywoof Crunchies

Blank Brand Dog Food

Doggy Delight

Healthy Pup Dog Food

Jake's Dog Food

Practicing Vocabulary

Choose the word from the box that best completes each analogy. Write the word on the line.

15. outdoor : indoor :: exterior : _____

16. velvety : touch :: _____ : taste

17. straight line : one way :: _____ : around

18. meager : poverty :: _____ : wealth

19. quest : search :: _____ : chase

20. rest : sleeping :: _____ : eating

21. seeing : scenery :: hearing : _____

circuit

interior

luxurious

nutrition

pursuit

scrumptious

voice-over

Writing an Advertisement
On another sheet of paper, write a radio or television advertisement for a product that pet owners might buy for their pets. When you have finished, share your work with a partner. Identify the persuasive devices in each other's work.

Literary Elements: Character

Understanding the characters in a story can help you comprehend the story as a whole. As you read, you can find clues to the characters' traits or personality characteristics. Some characters are confident; some are shy. Some characters are generous; others are mean-spirited.

There are several ways an author can show the traits of the characters in a story. What a character is like can be revealed by:

- **what the character *says***
- **what the character *does***
- **what the *narrator or other characters* say about the character**
- **how others *act* toward the character.**

Read the following story. As you read, look for clues that tell you about the characters.

"Hey, Alex," Marta said. "Do you want to work on our science project after school today?"

"I can't," answered Alex. "My grandfather is coming over to help me build a doghouse for Buster. We're going to construct it out of sod, the way the Nebraska pioneers built their homes."

"Why don't you tell him we have to work on the science project?" Marta asked.

"No, I promised I'd be home when he arrives, and I always keep my promises," Alex said. "Why don't you come over and help us? We can finish the science project on Saturday."

Marta grinned and nodded. "You have great ideas, Alex. It's a deal."

Fill in the circle next to all the answers that are correct.

Which of the following traits best describes Alex?

○ dishonest   ○ considerate

○ snobbish   ○ musical

How does the reader learn about Alex's character?

○ by what other characters say about him

○ by what he says and does

○ by how other characters act toward him

○ by what the narrator says about him

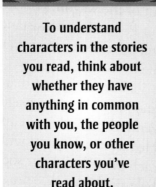

Tip

To understand characters in the stories you read, think about whether they have anything in common with you, the people you know, or other characters you've read about.

From the diary of
James Jacobsen

August 3, 1894

Dear Diary,

Today we had exceptional weather. We have made fine progress on our journey, but the trail is monotonous, and my feet are blistered from walking beside the wagon. Pa hopes we will be more prosperous in our new home in Nebraska than we were in the East. That hope is what keeps us going.

The Kelleys joined our wagon train last week. I have found a new friend in William Kelley, who shares my interest in fishing. Mama says she disapproves of William, though. He made quite a stir when he put a baby rattlesnake in Mrs. Kelley's laundry. The Kelleys plan to settle near Bellevue, Nebraska, which is our destination as well.

September 10, 1894

Dear Diary,

Tomorrow we begin work on the "soddy." Mama can't wait for it to be finished so that we can move out of the wagon. Poor Mama. I'd help her more, but Pa needs my assistance. Tomorrow my muscles will be tested as we cut and load blocks of sod for the house.

Pa has discovered that although our oxen did a fine job pulling the wagon all the way from Pennsylvania, they are too slow to cut sod properly. He has struck a deal with Mr. Kelley. We will help each other build our soddies. William Kelley will help us this week. I am glad, for he is the only boy near my age for miles around.

September 11, 1894

Dear Diary,

This morning Pa and I explored our claim for a good place to start cutting the sod.

I felt very proud when he listened respectfully to my views. William and I rode on the sod cutter as ballast while the Kelleys' horse pulled it along. Our weight makes the sod cutter cut through the thick prairie grass to make even bricks of sod. The roots are just deep enough to hold the dirt together. William and I were matched in strength as we piled the sod on a wheelbarrow and wheeled it back to the site of the soddy. When I went to the pump for a drink, William tipped the wheelbarrow, and some pieces of sod fell to the ground. Pa was furious with him, for we had to cut more sod to replace the broken pieces. He has been grumbling about going to help the Kelleys with their soddy next week.

September 30, 1894

Dear Diary,

Earlier this week we could see smoke in the distance. We were fearful that the wind might blow the fire in our direction across the dry prairie grass, but a rainstorm started and we were saved. We found out later that William Kelley had been playing with an oil lamp, and the dry branches and twigs on the roof of their new soddy caught fire. No one was injured, but Mama says William is a careless, tiresome boy.

Checking Comprehension

1. Do you think the Jacobsens could have built their home without the help of others? Explain.

   _____

2. How do you think the relationship between James and William might develop? What makes you think so?

   _____

   _____

Practicing Comprehension Skills

Put a checkmark in the box for each of the ways that the characters of James and William are revealed. Then write an example from the diary for each way you chose.

	James	William
3. By the character's own words	☐ _____ _____ _____	☐ _____ _____ _____
4. By the character's actions	☐ _____ _____ _____	☐ _____ _____ _____
5. By what others say about the character	☐ _____ _____ _____	☐ _____ _____ _____
6. By how others act toward the character	☐ _____ _____ _____	☐ _____ _____ _____

Complete the Venn diagram to compare James Jacobsen and William Kelley. In the left section, write two character traits that apply only to James. In the right section, write two character traits that apply only to William. In the middle section, write character traits that both boys share.

James	Both	William
7. _____	9. _____	11. _____
_____	_____	_____
8. _____	10. _____	12. _____
_____	_____	_____

Practicing Vocabulary

Choose a word from the box. Write it on the line next to the matching definition.

13. _____ doesn't admire

14. _____ boring, all the same

15. _____ extra weight

16. _____ excellent

17. _____ annoying

18. _____ goal

19. _____ successful

> **ballast**
>
> **destination**
>
> **disapproves**
>
> **exceptional**
>
> **monotonous**
>
> **prosperous**
>
> **tiresome**

Writing a Character Sketch

Try to recall an interesting character you read about in a book or story. What made that character memorable? On another sheet of paper, write a character sketch to show what the character is like. Be sure to reveal some of the character's traits through things he or she says and does, things the narrator or other characters say about the character, and your own descriptions.

Literary Elements: Plot

When you talk about the **plot** of a story, you're talking about the series of events that move the story forward. The chart below shows the parts of the plot.

Part of the Plot	Description
Background	information you need to know about the setting and characters
Conflict or problem	a struggle between two forces, whether between two or more characters or within an individual
Rising action	the events that build to the climax
Climax	where the characters face the conflict directly
Outcome or resolution	where the action winds down and the conflict is resolved

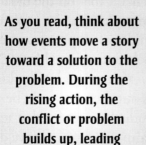

Think about the important elements of plot as you read the following story.

Captain Liang Tan had just finished inspecting the orbiting satellites. Her spaceship was finally headed home. Suddenly a control light warned that the ship's heat shield was loose. If Captain Tan went back into the Earth's atmosphere, her craft could explode.

She contacted Mission Control. "All functions are normal, Captain," the team reported. "Your control light must be in error. Proceed with reentry."

Captain Tan had flown with this control team since 2038, and she trusted them. Still, her pulse rate began climbing as she started the reentry engines.

The reentry went smoothly. At last the ship settled on the pad. Captain Tan was fine, but this had been the most difficult mission of her career.

What is the problem in this story?

_____

_____

List two events that are part of the story's rising action.

_____

_____

> ## Tip
>
> As you read, think about how events move a story toward a solution to the problem. During the rising action, the conflict or problem builds up, leading toward the story's climax and resolution.

As you read the following play, think about the different parts of the plot: background (setting and characters), problem, rising action, climax, and outcome or resolution.

Kids in Space

by Joyce Annette Barnes

Characters	
Captain	**Commander's Mom**
Commander	**Narrator**

Narrator: It is the year 2150. Two officers stand at the helm of a small but powerful spacecraft as it hurtles through the vast darkness of a faraway galaxy.

Commander *(speaking into a recording device)*: Commander's Log: It has been one hundred days since our launch from the International Space Station. We are the first kids in space, and our mission is to continue the search for new planets in the universe where humans can live. Captain, what is the status of our Reusable Launch Vehicle?

Captain: We're traveling at warp speed, and in two days we'll reach our destination planet. All systems are at peak level. Everything appears normal, Commander. In fact, the whole journey has been like a very long field trip. But—wait! What is that on the radar screen?

Commander *(peering at the control panel)*: An unidentified presence is on the screen. We've picked up a signal from 3,000 miles away. *(Looks out the window)* Who knows what's waiting for us out there? It could be anything! I wish I'd studied harder for that test on alien encounters!

Captain: What should we do, Commander?

Commander: Proceed with caution, Captain. We can't get distracted from our mission. Still, we must check this out and make sure it poses no threat to us.

Narrator: The engine slows as the spacecraft approaches the foreign object.

Captain: Commander, I can see something through the window now. It's a small light that looks vaguely familiar.

Commander: Yes, Captain. I have it in view. Look at that! It appears to be flashing like a neon light. Could it be—?

Captain *(excitedly)*: I don't know, Commander. There's no earthly reason for it.

Commander: It's a sign! I can't quite make out the letters. Captain, check it out with the Environmental Analyzer.

Captain: Yes, Commander! *(Pushes a button.)*

Narrator: The Captain sets off activity on an instrument panel. Within seconds, results flash on a computer screen.

(Both the Commander and the Captain react with delight, sniffing the air.)

Captain and Commander: It's a pizza restaurant! *(They give each other a high five.)*

Captain: All right! There *is* intelligent life in the universe!

Commander: Well, I don't think any harm will come if we stop for a couple of slices. Just one minute. *(Presses a button)* Mom?

Commander's Mom *(offstage voice)*: Yes, dear?

Commander: Can we get some pizza?

Commander's Mom: As long as you don't spoil your appetite for dinner.

Commander: Take her down, Captain.

Captain: Yes, Commander!

Checking Comprehension

1. In what ways are the Captain and Commander in this play like kids today?

    _____

    _____

2. Why do the Captain and Commander think there is intelligent life in the universe?

    _____

    _____

Practicing Comprehension Skills

3. Complete the diagram of *Kids in Space* by filling in the blank lines.

Background

Setting: _____

Main Characters: _____

Climax: _____

_____

_____

Rising Action: _____

_____

Problem: _____

_____

_____

Resolution: _____

_____

_____

List three events that lead the story to its climax.

4. _____

5. _____

6. _____

7. Circle the letter next to the sentence that states the story's climax.

    a. An unidentified presence is on the screen.   **b.** Is it possible, so far away from Earth?

    c. It's a pizza restaurant!   **d.** Yes, Commander!

8. Explain your answer to question 12 on the lines provided.

_____

_____

Practicing Vocabulary

Write the word from the box that belongs in each group.

9. steering mechanism, controlling position, _____

10. seems, looks, _____

11. speeds, rushes, _____

12. faintly, somewhat, _____

13. recyclable, can be used again, _____

14. possible, of this world, _____

15. not recognized, unknown, _____

appears
earthly
helm
hurtles
reusable
unidentified
vaguely

Writing a Science Fiction Story
Plan a science fiction story that takes place later in this century. It might be a space adventure or another type of futuristic tale. Prepare to write the story by identifying its setting, characters, problem, rising action, climax, and resolution. Outline your plot elements on another sheet of paper.

Literary Elements: Setting

The **setting** is the time and place in which a story occurs. Writers sometimes tell you exactly where and when the action takes place. At other times, a writer gives you clues about the setting through details. For example, if a story is set long ago, the author may tell about the characters traveling the countryside in a stagecoach pulled by horses. These details give you clues about where and when the events occur.

Setting can be an important part of the plot of a story. The setting often has an effect on what the characters do and what happens to them. The setting can also set up the **mood**, or feeling, of the story. A mood may be sad, dreamlike, eerie, or lighthearted, for instance. When you read a story, ask yourself, "Is the plot affected by the setting? Does the choice of setting help to create a mood? Could these same events occur in a different time or in a different place?"

Read the following story. Pay special attention to details that describe setting. Ask yourself how the setting affects the events and the characters.

The Civil War was over at last. Many former slaves took their dreams of freedom and opportunity to the Wild West. In 1865, Eddie Perkins was only fourteen years old. Newly freed, Eddie left the Georgia plantation where he'd spent his childhood and found work as a cowboy in Kansas.

Eddie's work as a cowboy was very demanding. He spent days and nights in the saddle as he tended huge herds of cattle on the open range. The work was also dangerous as he faced wild animals and outlaws.

Eddie enjoyed his work and became well-known for his skills. By 1875 he had won a riding, roping, and shooting contest in a town in the Dakota Territory called Ready, earning him the nickname of "Ready Eddie."

Where and when does this story take place?

_____

_____

Think about how setting affected Eddie's story. How would a cowboy's life be different in 1975 instead of 1875?

_____

_____

_____

Tip

Remember that setting means both when and where a story takes place. The time and place in which a story is set can sometimes have an effect on the characters, the plot, and the mood.

Read the following adventure story. Identify the setting and think about how it affects the events of the story.

Day Hike

"Turn here!" said my sister Rosa as our car neared Mount Benton. "This place looks great!" she shrieked as we parked in front of the lodge.

In winter, the lodge was snowbound, but now, in May, the rocky ground was only spotted with ice. The sun sparkled on a lake nestled behind the lodge. The smooth surface of the water reflected the mountain as well as some puffy clouds in the sky. Paul directed Rosa and me into the lodge, where we signed the hikers' log. Paul listed exactly the trail we would take to Lookout Point, noting that we planned to return by about 2:00 P.M.

Rosa had chattered constantly during our entire trip. She was thrilled about this wilderness trek with our favorite uncle. At 24, Paul was nine years older than my sister and 12 years older than I was.

The hike was Paul's idea. He thought that a wilderness experience would help bring us closer.

I was not as excited about this hike as the others. The "great outdoors" makes me kind of nervous. I was willing to go along with Paul and Rosa and hope for the best, though I'd been reading up on survival skills just in case.

As we were about to leave, the park ranger warned, "Storm clouds are forecast. If they move in, you'd better head down. It gets cold very fast."

Paul assured him that we would be careful, and we started up the trail. We quickly shed our jackets. Paul cracked jokes, and Rosa asked me questions about the various plants and animal tracks we saw along the trail. As we climbed, the air thinned. We donned our jackets once again. I got a little dizzy

from altitude sickness, so I rested, drank some water, and felt better.

"Look at nature's spectacle!" Paul exclaimed as he swept his arm across the view.

What I noticed was quickly changing weather. Clouds began obscuring the sights.

"Check out those clouds, Paul," I said.

"We're in the mountains, Ramon!" he answered matter-of-factly. "We're just closer to the clouds."

We kept going. At Lookout Point there wasn't much looking out to do. By then it was a white world of clouds, fog, and now, a blizzard. Suddenly Paul seemed eager to descend. We followed wordlessly until he stopped.

"I can't see," Paul called, sounding more worried and uncertain than I liked. "I've lost the trail."

I felt more confident now, because I recalled advice from my survival book. "We should stay put," I said firmly. "There's no sense roaming around in circles. When we don't return on time, the patrols will search for us."

Paul and Rosa didn't argue. We huddled together, shared trail mix, and talked.

By 4:00, a patrol found us and soon zoomed us down the trail on their snowmobiles.

I guess Uncle Paul got his wish. That hike really did bring the three of us closer together!

Checking Comprehension

1. What happened that put the three hikers in danger?

    _____

    _____

2. Why was the patrol able to rescue the hikers?

    _____

    _____

Practicing Comprehension Skills

3. Where and when does this story take place?

    _____

4. What details from the story tell the setting?

    _____

5. How do you think the story would change if it were set 100 years ago?

    _____

    _____

Fill in the circle before the correct answer.

6. How did the setting affect the mood of the story?
    - ○ The appearance of the lodge made the story feel sad.
    - ○ The snow falling on the mountain trail made the mood tense.
    - ○ Rosa's chatter in the car made the mood joyous.
    - ○ The setting did not affect the mood of the story at all.

7. Which of the following details does not tell more about the mountain setting?
    - ○ the view from Lookout Point   ○ the plants and animals
    - ○ the car   ○ the trail

Use the chart below to explain how the weather on the trail affected Paul's and Ramon's behavior in different ways. Write your answers on the lines provided.

Effect of weather on Paul's behavior	Effect of weather on Ramon's behavior
8. _____ _____ _____ _____ _____	9. _____ _____ _____ _____ _____ _____

Practicing Vocabulary

10. Choose the word from the box that best completes each blank in the paragraph. Write the word on the line.

altitude	donned	hikers'	huddled	log	nature's	obscuring

"From the top of this mountain, you'll see _____ finest entertainment!" our guide said as he signed the _____ . "We have great weather, and there's no danger of fog _____ the trail." We all _____ our hats as protection from the sun. As we started to climb the mountain, another group of hikers began to descend it. We met that group at the halfway point and _____ around the _____ leader. She warned us that the high _____ might make us feel faint as we continued our climb.

Writing a Narrative Paragraph
Think about an outdoor adventure you have had, or make up one that sounds exciting. On a separate sheet of paper, write a narrative paragraph about the adventure. Make the setting clear by stating when and where the story takes place and by including details that reveal the time and place.

Literary Elements: Theme

Most fiction writers have a "big idea" in mind when they write a story. This "big idea" that the writer wants you to know is called the story's theme. Some themes are directions for living life, such as "Don't sweat the small stuff." Other themes are observations about the world, such as "Appearances can be deceiving." A story's theme is not always stated directly. Sometimes you must figure it out for yourself. Often you can use skills such as drawing conclusions to help you.

Some stories will have one major theme, as well as one or more minor themes. A story about a character who finds a lost puppy, wishes she could keep it, and decides to find the rightful owner might have a major theme of "Honesty is the best policy." A minor theme in the story might be "Don't bite off more than you can chew" when the character has trouble finding the owner because she neglects to ask anyone for help.

Read the following story. As you read, think about the theme the author is trying to communicate.

Molly woke up early. She'd been looking forward to the field trip to the animal shelter ever since Mr. Bernstein had announced it.

"Sometimes," Mr. Bernstein had said, "people do not respect animals as living things. They purchase a little bunny or kitten because they think it's cute. When the animal gets bigger and isn't quite as cuddly or eats too much food, the owner doesn't want it anymore. Then some people just let the animal go, expecting it to be able to fend for itself." Mr. Bernstein hoped that his students would learn to treat animals responsibly.

Put a checkmark next to the sentence that best states the theme of this passage.

_____ Everyone should have a pet.

_____ Teachers who care are the best teachers.

_____ Many animals are abandoned or mistreated.

_____ Animals are living beings and should be treated with respect.

What might be a minor theme in this passage?

_____

Tip

As you look for the theme of a story, ask yourself, "What is the author's 'big idea'? What is the message that could be applied to other stories or to my own life?"

Read the following story. As you read, think about the theme, or the "big idea" the author is communicating.

Secrets of the Swamp

Leotie Johnson knew something most twelve-year-olds did not know: she knew about orchids. Her family grew them and shipped them all over the world.

Leotie's father had taken her on several orchid-finding trips in the swamplands near their Florida home. This time they were looking for a species so rare, some people thought it was extinct. Commonly called the ghost orchid, it bloomed only once a year. The ghost orchid had no leaves at all; its roots wrapped themselves around a tree. The flower was a beautiful papery white, and the side petals tapered into long, fluttery tails.

When they set off, Leotie had been excited at the prospect of finding the ghost orchid, but she was growing irritable from the insects and the intense humidity. As she walked—or rather, sloshed—through the swamp in her snake-proof boots, her legs ached and her head hurt. She felt miserable.

She kept her eyes open for alligators and snakes. These swamps had both. Though her father had taught her how to protect herself if she were ever threatened by an alligator or a poisonous snake, she certainly didn't want to encounter one.

Suddenly her dad signaled her to stop. A few feet ahead, basking on a tree limb, was a four-foot-long snake. Leotie froze. The snake had the brown coloration and thick body of the poisonous cottonmouth.

"Think, Leotie," her father said calmly. "Look at its face."

Leotie forced herself to take a good look at the snake. No dark brown band ran across the side of its head. "It's a water snake," she said, breathing again as the harmless snake slithered down the tree and disappeared under the water.

"Plenty of water snakes die every year because people think they're cottonmouths. They don't take a moment to look. They just react with fear and kill a snake that has a right to be left alone in its native habitat."

As they continued their slow trek through the swamp, Leotie's dad stopped abruptly and said excitedly, "There! The ghost orchid! Isn't it beautiful?"

Leotie stared in awe at the pure white orchid, set against the dark bark. Instinctively, she reached out to touch the white petals, then picked up her camera instead. "Dad, will growers ever be able to cultivate them?" she asked.

"Well, Leotie, I don't know. These plants are endangered, so it's against the law to collect them from the wild. All we can do is take some pictures."

"Even if we can never grow them," Leotie said, "we'll always have the memory of seeing at least one!"

Checking Comprehension

1. What do you know about Leotie and her family from reading this story?

    _____

    _____

    _____

2. Why did Leotie leave the snake alone?

    _____

    _____

    _____

Practicing Comprehension Skills

3. What do you think the main theme is in "Secrets of the Swamp"?

    _____

4. Give some details from the story that support the theme you identified.

    _____

    _____

    _____

5. Put a checkmark next to the sentence that expresses a minor theme of the story.

    _____ Cottonmouths and water snakes are often confused.

    _____ Swamps are very humid and uncomfortable.

    _____ Sharing common interests can bring parents and children closer together.

    _____ Some orchids are very rare.

6. If Leotie had expressed another minor theme of the story in dialogue, which of the following might she have said?

- ○ "I'm so hot and tired, Dad. Let's go home."
- ○ "Snakes make me very nervous."
- ○ "I wish the day would come when growers can cultivate orchids."
- ○ "Finding the orchid was worth all the trouble. I'm glad we didn't give up."

7. Think about the theme of this story. Could you apply it to other situations or other stories you have read? Explain.

_____

_____

_____

Practicing Vocabulary

Write a word from the box to complete each sentence.

| abruptly | basking | cultivate | encounter | humidity | irritable | miserable |

8. When the _____ is high, there is a lot of moisture in the air.

9. Sweltering summer days can seem _____ if you are not used to the heat.

10. Because snakes are cold-blooded, you will often find them _____ in the sun for warmth.

11. To _____, or raise, orchids requires dedication and knowledge.

12. After three hours of walking, some hikers began to get _____ .

13. The group heard a strange noise and _____ stopped to look around.

14. No one wants to _____ a dangerous animal when hiking.

Writing a Realistic Story
Think about a theme you would like to express to others. On another sheet of paper, write a realistic story that expresses your theme. Decide whether you want to state the theme in your story or let your readers figure it out for themselves.

Synonyms

Think about these two sentences:

The stubborn dog refused to move an inch.

The determined dog refused to move an inch.

The words *stubborn* and *determined* are synonyms, but each has a slightly different meaning. Careful writers choose just the right word for each situation. **Synonyms** are useful because they are words with similar, though not usually identical, meanings. The right synonym is the one that will best convey the writer's meaning, mood, and tone.

Notice synonyms as you read and think about why the author has chosen them. The synonyms can change the intensity, strength, seriousness, or other characteristics of the people, place, things, and actions being described. They can also help a writer to avoid repeating the same words.

Read the following paragraphs. As you read, notice synonyms that are used and think about how they create specific meanings.

Guide dogs lead blind or visually impaired people on streets, in stores and offices, and other places. These dogs must be strong and healthy, with friendly, calm, and confident personalities. They must also be intelligent, recognizing situations in which they should disobey their handlers.

Imagine that a dog and handler are walking down a sidewalk when suddenly the dog sits down. The person commands the guide dog to go forward, but the dog refuses. When the person insists, the dog still does not obey. Instead it pushes the person away. Why didn't the dog follow the command? A car is backing out of a driveway in front of the pair. Dog and handler are a team—a partnership built on trust and love.

Find a synonym in the second paragraph for the word "obey." Why do you think the author chose not to use "obey" twice?

_____

In the last two sentences, how are the meanings of *pair, team,* and *partnership* alike or different?

_____

_____

_____

Tip

Synonyms are words with similar, though not usually identical, meanings. Synonyms can change the strength, seriousness, or other characteristics of the people, places, things, or actions being described.

As you read the following article, look for synonyms and think about how they show the author's exact meaning.

Puppy People

Imagine taking an adorable puppy into your family. You love and train it throughout its first year, knowing that at the end of the year, you'll have to give it up. That's just what puppy raisers do. Puppy raisers raise guide dogs for blind and visually impaired people.

When a potential guide dog puppy is about eight weeks old, it goes to live with a family, sleeping inside the house as a member of the family. It's fine if the family has lots of children or other pets, since a guide dog needs to learn how to behave no matter who or what else is around.

The puppy raiser's responsibility is not to turn the puppy into a guide dog, but to make the dog a well-behaved family member. That means someone must spend quality time with the puppy, including playing with it and patting, grooming, and training it. Training the puppy involves housebreaking it, not permitting it to chew shoes or furniture, and encouraging it to be quiet and calm.

Guide dogs take blind people into a complex world. There are many distractions that could keep the dog from working. The puppy raiser helps the puppy become socialized, or well-behaved in groups, by exposing it to lots of new environments and praising it when it stays calm. Visits to the park, mall, and bus stop are all valuable field trips for the puppy. Since guide dogs may have to travel in cars, buses, planes, ferries, and other vehicles, puppy raisers try to give their puppies useful experiences of this nature too. Many puppy raisers even take their puppies to work with them. Learning to be calm and disciplined in a work situation is important for a guide dog.

Although the puppy raiser is not responsible for training the puppy to be a guide dog, the puppy can be taught simple commands. Daily training sessions teach the dog such easy commands as "Sit," "Down," and "Stay." The one command the puppy is not taught is "Heel," because a guide dog stands in front of the handler, not at the handler's side.

Dogs love to eat, but it is crucial for future guide dogs to learn to dine only from their own bowls. They cannot be distracted by the sight and smells of food while they are working, so there can be no begging at the table and no handouts from strangers.

When the dog is between a year and eighteen months old, the puppy raiser's job is over. The dog is now ready to do its real work. The family members have committed their time, energy, and care. When their work is done, they always feel sad to give up the dog they have loved so much. They can do it only because they know someone else needs the dog more than they do.

Checking Comprehension

1. Why is it so important for a guide dog to learn to be calm and well-behaved?

   _____

2. Would you like to be a puppy raiser? Why or why not?

   _____

   _____

Practicing Comprehension Skills

Match the words from the article "Puppy People" on the left with their synonyms
on the right by writing the correct letter in the blank space.

——— 3. disciplined   a. useful

——— 4. eat   b. easy

——— 5. valuable   c. well-behaved

——— 6. over   d. dine

——— 7. simple   e. done

Choose the synonym that best completes the sentence. Write it in the blank.

8. I work with my puppy every day to _____ her simple commands.

   educate   teach   instruct

9. It's important for a dog to avoid distractions while he is _____ .

   working   employed   active

10. Taking the puppy on a plane provided a valuable _____ for her.

   occurrence   experience   adventure

11. How is a potential guide dog like and unlike a future guide dog?

   _____

   _____

The author of "Puppy People" uses the word *calm* and its synonym *quiet*. What other words have meanings similar to *calm*? Brainstorm synonyms or find them in a thesaurus. Organize them in the synonym web below so that the most similar words are grouped together in the same spoke.

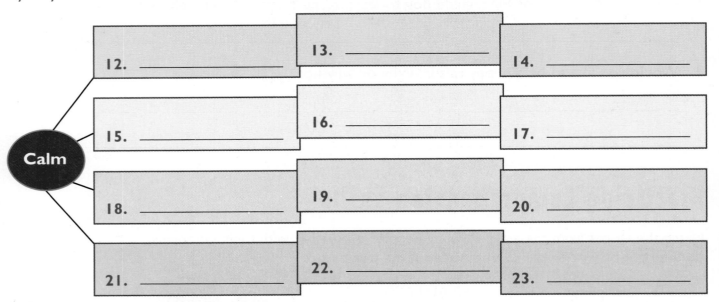

12. _____

13. _____

14. _____

15. _____

16. _____

17. _____

18. _____

19. _____

20. _____

21. _____

22. _____

23. _____

Calm

Practicing Vocabulary

Choose the word from the box that is a synonym for each word listed below.
Write the synonym on the line.

24. _____ allowing

25. _____ important

26. _____ interruptions

27. _____ complicated

28. _____ charming

29. _____ showing

30. _____ devoted

adorable

committed

complex

crucial

distractions

exposing

permitting

Writing a Description
Think about a pet you know—your own or someone else's. On another piece of paper, write a paragraph that describes the pet's physical traits and personality. Use a thesaurus to choose the most precise words you can find.

Antonyms

Antonyms are words with opposite meanings, such as *hot* and *cold*, *top* and *bottom*, *wise* and *foolish*. When an author points out contrasts between ideas, characters, settings, or other things, you can expect to find antonyms.

The prefixes *un-*, *in-*, *dis-*, and *im-* can change words into their antonyms. For example, *able* and *unable*, *decisive* and *indecisive*, *trust* and *distrust*, and *possible* and *impossible* are all antonyms.

Pay attention to antonyms in the stories and articles you read. They can help you understand how characters, ideas, or other things are different.

Read the diary entry below. Notice how antonyms give opposite meanings.

Sunday, April 12

Dear Diary,

I just returned from my visit with Jenny. When she moved away, we promised to be best friends forever, but she's changed so much! Jenny and I were once so similar, but this weekend, we seemed very different.

We spent the whole weekend playing quiet games instead of our usual noisy fun. She doesn't even like basketball anymore! When it was time to go home, I left eagerly rather than reluctantly. I felt unhappy at first, but then Mom said it was normal for friendships to change. I'm sure glad Beverly moved into our building last week!

Reread the diary entry to find the antonym for each word listed below. Write the antonym on the line.

different   _____

quiet   _____

eagerly   _____

unhappy   _____

Choose two antonym pairs from the list above. Change one word so that the pair still shows antonyms. For example, if the antonym pair were *hot/cold*, other antonym pairs could be *hot/cool* or *warm/cold*.

_____

_____

Tip

Some negative prefixes, such as *dis-*, *un-*, *in-*, and *im-*, turn base words into their antonyms. When you see a word with a negative prefix, think about its antonym to figure out the meaning.

Read the following story. Notice the contrasts that are pointed out with antonyms.

The Other Mr. Franklin

Denise passed by and waved to her neighbor Mr. Franklin as he packed his car with two big suitcases. "He must be going on a long trip," Denise decided as he waved back. She thought no more about it until two days later, when she noticed that Mr. Franklin's back door was open. "Thieves!" thought Denise, but then she saw Mr. Franklin emerge from the doorway. "It's peculiar," Denise thought, "that he packed so much for such a short trip."

Denise waved to Mr. Franklin, but he didn't wave back, which certainly seemed out of the ordinary. Mr. Franklin had always been cordial. Not waving seemed almost unfriendly.

After school the next day, Denise saw Mr. Franklin working on the new shelves in his garage. His cat was in the front yard. It was very unusual for the cat to be outdoors.

"Hello, Mr. Franklin," Denise said.

"Hello to you, young lady," he replied.

"Is everything okay with you?" asked Denise.

"I'd say that everything's just right!" said Mr. Franklin.

That night Denise told her mother, "Something is wrong with Mr. Franklin."

"Is he ill?" asked her mother.

"He seems healthy, but he's just not himself."

"I've got the answer," offered Denise's brother, Ray. "We read a story about something like this in school. A normal guy went through another dimension, and he started acting really abnormal. Even his dog didn't recognize him."

"I don't think that's the problem," Denise said, "but I do feel as if I'd met another Mr. Franklin."

The next day, Denise saw Mr. Franklin get into his car. "Didn't Mr. Franklin's old car used to be a dull red?" she asked. "That one is so bright."

"Maybe he bought a new car," said Denise's mother. "Sometimes there's a simple explanation for things that seem complicated."

Denise couldn't stop thinking about Mr. Franklin's strange behavior. In her imagination, the neighbor she had known was the genuine Mr. Franklin, and this new neighbor was the false Mr. Franklin. False Mr. Franklin had a hurried gait; genuine Mr. Franklin strolled in a leisurely way. Genuine Mr. Franklin always wore a hat; false Mr. Franklin never wore one. Genuine Mr. Franklin watered his garden in the morning; false Mr. Franklin watered in the evening. Something seemed wrong.

Two weeks later, Mr. Franklin rang the doorbell. He held out a wrapped parcel and said, "This is a gift from my wonderful trip to Africa." Denise knew this was the genuine Mr. Franklin.

"Did you meet my brother?" Mr. Franklin asked. "He house-sat for me while I was gone."

"Ah…are you and your brother identical twins, by any chance?" asked Denise.

"Ever since the day we were born," said Mr. Franklin.

"Then I *did* meet the other Mr. Franklin," Denise said with a smile.

Checking Comprehension

1. Why is Denise concerned about her neighbor?

   _____

   _____

2. How do you think Denise feels at the end of the story?

   _____

   _____

Practicing Comprehension Skills

Read the word in the center circle. Fill in each surrounding circle with an antonym from the story.

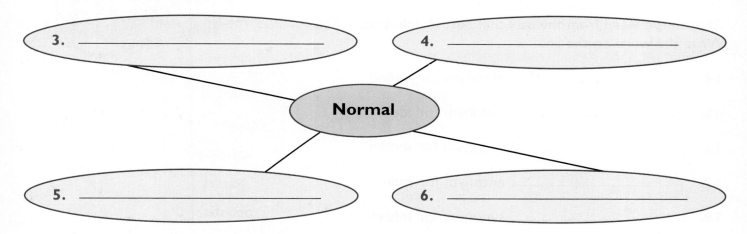

3. _____   4. _____

Normal

5. _____   6. _____

Fill in the circle next to the antonym for the underlined word.

7. The solution to the mystery was <u>simple</u> rather than _____ .

   ○ brief   ○ wide   ○ complicated   ○ hopeful

8. Denise thought that Mr. Franklin was <u>healthy</u>, not _____ .

   ○ healthful   ○ genuine   ○ ill   ○ ordinary

9. Mr. Franklin's car was <u>bright</u> red instead of _____ red.

   ○ new   ○ shiny   ○ red   ○ dull

Complete each analogy with an antonym from the story:

10. *lengthy* is to *brief* as *long* is to _____ .

    edge   endless   short

11. *Often* is to *rarely* as *always* is to _____ .

    generally   never   usually

12. *Error* is to *correction* as *wrong* is to _____ .

    right   incorrect   dull

13. *Worn* is to *fresh* as *old* is to _____ .

    false   real   new

Practicing Vocabulary

Choose the word from the box that best matches each clue.
Write the word on the line.

14. _____ antonym for *rushed*

15. _____ synonym for *racks*

16. _____ synonym for *reason*

17. _____ antonym for *rude*

18. _____ synonym for *robbers*

19. _____ antonym for *common*

20. _____ synonym for *package*

| cordial |
| explanation |
| leisurely |
| parcel |
| peculiar |
| shelves |
| thieves |

Writing a Contrast Essay
Use another piece of paper to write about two people, animals, places,
or things that are opposites in some ways. Use antonyms to point out
differences.

Using Figurative Language

We call expressions that can't be understood from the usual, everyday definitions of their words **figurative language**. Writers often use such expressions to give a clearer picture of what they mean. There are several types of figurative language.

Type of Language	Definition	Example
simile	a comparison of unlike things using words such as *like* or *as*	Young Hercules wrestled *like a lion cub.*
metaphor	a comparison of unlike things without any words of comparison	With his *muscles of iron* Hercules defeated each enemy.
idiom	a phrase that cannot be understood using ordinary definitions	He refused to *back down* from his enemies.
personification	giving human characteristics to animals or things	The golden apples *winked* in the sunlight.
hyperbole	an exaggeration that is used for emphasis	Hercules was *so hungry he could eat a horse.*

Read the following Greek myth. Notice how descriptive expressions help create a picture.

Hera, the queen of the gods, was jealous of the mighty Hercules. She forced Hercules to serve a wicked king. To win his freedom, Hercules had to perform 12 difficult tasks called *labors*.

Task eleven was for Hercules to collect some golden apples as bright as the sun. Near the apple orchard, Hercules found Atlas, a giant who supported the heavy sky on his shoulders. "I'll get the apples for you," Atlas said, "but you must hold up the sky."

Hercules suspected that Atlas had a trick up his sleeve. When Atlas had fetched the apples, Hercules said, "Take the sky back for a moment while I make a cushion for my shoulder." As Atlas took back the sky, Hercules picked up the apples and ran away at lightning speed.

In the passage above, find examples of the following types of figurative language and write them on the lines provided.

Simile: _____

Idiom: _____

Hyperbole: _____

Tip

As you read, pay attention to figurative language. Think about why the author chose to use a certain expression. Try to form a mental picture of the person or thing being described.

Read the following story. Look for figurative language the author uses. Use the description to form a picture in your mind.

The Labors of Stacy

by Norma Johnston

"Playing Hercules in *The Labors of Hercules* will be Stewart Potter," Mrs. Minter announced, "and the narrator, Athene, will be Roxie Grant."

Stacy ducked her head as waves of disappointment crashed over her. She didn't even get a part! "It's no big deal," she told herself—but the play, the culmination of the annual sixth-grade Greek and Roman festival, *was* a big deal. When the bell sounded, everyone else in her language arts class stampeded for the door.

Mrs. Minter sat down next to Stacy. "I know you're disappointed," she said gently, "but I really need you for something more important: props manager. You can ask other students to assist you— Greg's already volunteered."

Stacy swallowed hard. "I'll do the best I can, I promise."

To Stacy's surprise, "running props" was fun. With gold paint, Stacy and Greg transformed garbage pail lids into shields. They covered football and bicycle helmets with gold and silver foil. Best of all, Stacy and Greg made enormous mythological monsters out of craft paper and mounted them on poles. The monsters grimaced and smirked as they swooped around the stage.

When she wasn't making props, Stacy attended rehearsals. Stewart didn't know his lines, and Stacy prompted him so often she knew them by heart.

By the day of the play, everyone had the jitters. At the dress rehearsal, watching Stewart clowning around as usual, Mrs. Minter looked as grave as a judge.

"Stewart, watch that pole!" she said sharply— seconds before Stewart tripped. The cast stared in horror as Stewart lay groaning on the stage.

"I need to help Stewart," Mrs. Minter announced succinctly. She suspended the rehearsal by saying, "I'll see the rest of you at six."

By six o'clock, neither Stewart nor Mrs. Minter was in the classroom. Everyone fell silent when Mrs. Minter walked in alone. "Stewart won't be able to perform tonight," she said.

"What about our play?" someone blurted. "No one else knows Hercules' lines."

"Stacy does," Greg said placidly.

"A girl playing Hercules?" Roxie drawled.

"Why not?" Greg inquired. "Stacy knows the play inside out."

"Will you do it, Stacy?" Mrs. Minter asked.

Stacy nodded weakly.

After donning her costume, Stacy hardly recognized herself inside Hercules' beard and helmet. Once she was out on the stage, the play claimed her completely. When she pulled off her artificial beard during curtain call, everybody gasped. Applause and cheers rained on her.

Stacy changed and was walking outside to meet her parents when a voice said, "Hey, you were good!" She jumped. It was Stewart, on crutches.

"Thanks," said Stacy dryly. "What are you doing here?"

"Wild horses couldn't drag me away— not even the ones Hercules tamed." He gave her a smile and a wink; then he was gone. Stacy rolled her eyes and ran toward her waiting parents.

Checking Comprehension

1. Which character takes the school play more seriously, Stacy or Stewart? Explain your answer.

   _____

   _____

2. How does Stewart's injury affect Stacy's contribution to the play?

   _____

   _____

Practicing Comprehension Skills

Fill in the circle that names the type of figurative language shown by the words in italics.

3. Stacy knows the play *by heart*.

   ○ idiom　　　　○ hyperbole　　　　○ metaphor　　　　○ simile

4. Stacy *hardly recognized herself* inside Hercules' beard and helmet.

   ○ personification　　○ idiom　　　　○ metaphor　　　　○ hyperbole

5. Fill in the circle next to the example of personification.

   ○ Stacy ducked her head.　　　　　　○ Everyone else in her language arts class stampeded for the door.

   ○ Stacy and Greg transformed garbage pail lids into shields.　　　　○ The monsters grimaced and smirked as they swooped around the stage.

Identify the types of figurative language in the following sentences and tell what each expression means.

6. "Stacy knows the play inside out." _____

   _____

7. "Wild horses couldn't drag me away."

   _____

   _____

Look at the following sentences. On the blank line, write an **M** if the sentence is an example of a metaphor and an **S** if the sentence is an example of a simile. Circle the things the simile or metaphor is comparing. The first example has been completed for you.

8. __M__ (Waves) of (disappointment) crashed over her.

9. ____ Mrs. Minter looked as grave as a judge.

10. ____ Applause and cheers rained on her.

11. ____ Everyone in class stampeded for the door.

Practicing Vocabulary

Choose a word from the box that best replaces the underlined word or words. Write the word on the left.

culmination	grave	grimaced	placidly	stampeded	succinctly	suspended

12. _____ When the tickets went on sale, the fans <u>rushed to</u> the box office.

13. _____ The <u>highest point</u> of weeks of rehearsing came when the audience stood and cheered.

14. _____ Stacy <u>frowned</u> at the thought of Stewart's injury.

15. _____ Although everyone else seemed worried, the director spoke <u>calmly</u>.

16. _____ The critic's short review <u>briefly</u> summarized the performance.

17. _____ The teacher looked <u>serious and concerned</u> as she announced the problem.

18. _____ After the blizzard, school was <u>temporarily closed</u> for two days.

Writing a Descriptive Paragraph
On another sheet of paper, write a paragraph that describes a time when you performed in public. Perhaps you performed in a play or a recital, competed in a sports event, or made a presentation. To help your readers picture the event and understand your feelings, use at least three examples of figurative language.

Analogies

Do you know what an **analogy** is? It is a comparison. An analogy shows that a relationship between one pair of words is similar to the relationship between another pair. For example, the relationship between *big* and *large* is similar to the relationship between *small* and *tiny* because both pairs are **synonyms**. The comparison can be expressed with words or with dots. The dots stand for the words *is to* and *as*.

big is to *large* as *small* is to *tiny*   **big** : *large* :: *small* : *tiny*

Analogies can show many different relationships in addition to showing synonyms. Some more of those relationships can be found in the chart below.

Opposites	Cause and Effect
summer : winter :: hot : cold	ice : slip :: sun : burn
Categories	**Part-to-Whole**
canary : bird :: poodle : dog	branch : tree :: nose : face

Read this paragraph about tarantulas. Look for an analogy.

If you are a mouse, you want to stay out of the way of a tarantula. That's because a tarantula is to a mouse as a fox is to a chicken. A tarantula comes out at night to hunt. Because it has poor vision, a tarantula searches for its victims by touch. When a tarantula finds a tasty meal, it bites its victim and releases a paralyzing venom with its large fangs. A tarantula's bite is not deadly to humans, but it does hurt.

Write a cause-and-effect analogy you found in the paragraph.

_____

On the line, write the word that completes the analogy. Then, in each box, identify the kind of analogy you have completed.

sleeves : shirt :: wings : _____

engine   airplane   clothes

sweater : clothing :: dictionary : _____

book   library   store

sweet : sour :: soft : _____

tart   sugary   hard

Tip

To figure out what an analogy means, you must figure out the relationship between the first pair of words. Then compare the second pair using the same relationship.

Read a story about a boy who finds a tarantula. Look for analogies as you read.

Rain Forest Discoveries

Jason peered outside his wooden hut into the darkness of the rain forest's dense growth. The night was as dark as the day had been bright. However, the darkness couldn't dim his happiness at being on vacation in South America with his father.

Jason ran his fingers over the inside of the mosquito netting that surrounded his bed. Then he saw a small, furry, brown spider slowly climbing the wall beside his bed.

His father was snoring in the bed next to him. Jason tiptoed over to the bureau, not wanting to disturb the spider or wake his father. He picked up his father's empty eyeglass case, very slowly moved it above the creature's body, and scooped it up. Now he would have his very own South American pet, a native tarantula.

The next day, Jason and his father were on the river at dawn to see the macaws at the clay bank. Hundreds of these large parrots with blue, green, yellow, and red feathers clung to the clay bank, and Jason watched them with fascination. They flew about and shrieked loudly when provoked. The sight was spectacular, and it was lunchtime before they returned to the hut. Jason immediately checked inside the eyeglass box, but it was empty!

He looked everywhere in the room, in the shower next door, and on the porch outside.

"What are you looking for?" Jason's father asked.

"Um, well," Jason hedged. He was not sure his father would approve of his new acquisition. His father treasured nature the way Jason treasured his coin collection.

"A tarantula, perhaps?" Jason's dad pointed to the spider crawling on the rafter above.

Jason reached up to touch it, but his dad stopped him. "I wouldn't grab that if I were you!" he said. "If that spider gets frightened, it might give you a nasty bite."

"My friend Alex has a tarantula that doesn't bite."

"Alex's tarantula is probably tame. This spider lives in the jungle."

"You mean I can't take it home with me?"

"Think about it. Is it better off here in the rain forest, or locked up in your bedroom?"

Jason thought about his room back home and gazed out at the forest. His father's earnestness convinced him. He said, "I guess I was being thoughtless. To a tarantula, our house would be the same as a prison is to a person."

"Good thinking, Jason," his dad said.

Jason gently placed a piece of cardboard under the spider and ushered it to the safety of a large leaf on the edge of the forest. The spider slowly walked to freedom.

Checking Comprehension

1. Why does Jason agree to let the tarantula go?

_____

_____

2. Why do you think Jason wanted to keep the tarantula as a pet?

_____

_____

Practicing Comprehension Skills

Read the incomplete analogies below. On the line, write the word that completes the analogy. Then, in each box, identify the kind of analogy you have completed: synonyms, categories, opposites, cause and effect, or part-to-whole.

3. empty : full :: big : _____

   container   enormous   small

4. pine forest : North America :: _____ : South America

   wood   macaws   rain forest

5. macaw : parrot :: collie : _____

   dog   insect   doghouse

6. tarantula : bite :: bee: _____

   eat   sting   venom

7. remember: _____ :: bother : disturb

   recall   sameness   forget

8. dawn : sun :: _____ : moon

   morning   evening   clock

9. Finish this analogy from "Rain Forest Discoveries." Then explain what it means.

house : _____ :: prison : person

_____

Express the following sentences from "Rain Forest Discoveries" as analogies.

10. The night was as dark as the day had been bright.

_____

11. His father treasured nature the way Jason treasured his coin collection.

_____

Practicing Vocabulary

Use the words in the box to fill in the blank in each sentence.

acquisition	earnestness	fascination	happiness	hedged	provoked	ushered

12. Jason _____ the spider to its freedom.

13. He wondered if his father would like his new _____ , the tarantula.

14. Because he didn't know how to answer his dad, Jason _____ his reply.

15. They watched in _____ as the macaws flapped their bright wings.

16. Jason took coin collecting seriously, and his father treated the subject of nature with the same _____ .

17. Jason felt intense _____ when he learned he was going on the trip.

18. When the macaws shrieked, you knew something must have _____ them.

Writing a Description
On another sheet of paper, write a paragraph that describes something in nature. In your description, make several comparisons. When you finish, write one of the comparisons as an analogy.

Connotation and Denotation

Imagine that you are about to take a test that is described as *difficult*. You might think to yourself that the test is very hard. Now imagine that the same test is described as *challenging*. Perhaps to you a *challenging* test is an interesting one that brings out your best abilities. Although *difficult* and *challenging* mean nearly the same thing, they suggest different ideas.

We call a dictionary meaning of a word its **denotation**. We call the ideas or feelings you may associate with that word its **connotation**. While the denotation of a word will be the same for everyone, its connotation can change.

Connotations can be **positive** (thinking or feeling that something is good) or **negative** (thinking or feeling that something is bad). Context clues can tell you whether an author meant for a word to have positive or negative connotations. Connotations can also change according to a reader's experiences. In the example above, *difficult* has a negative connotation, while *challenging* has a positive one.

As you read the following passage, think about how word connotations affect the message.

Tina and Ana needed to perform volunteer work as part of a project. Because both girls had good grades in math, they decided to tutor young children in the neighborhood. Tina wrote this notice.

Tutoring by Tina and Ana

Do your children need more practice with math skills? We can help most school kids do well. At the end of each meeting, we will test your child's progress.

"I have a few changes to suggest," Ana said. After she changed some words, the notice read:

Do your children need practice with math skills? We can help most students excel. At the end of each meeting, we will evaluate your child's work.

> **Tip**
>
> While the denotation of a word can be found in a dictionary, a word's connotation cannot. A connotation is more personal and can be influenced by your own experience.

Read each of the following sentences. Underline the words in parentheses that have the more positive connotation.

We can help most (school kids, students) (do well, excel).

At the end of each meeting, we will (evaluate, test) your child's (progress, work).

Read the following story. As you read, think about the connotation and denotation of some of the words.

The Quiz Show

It was a dismal, rainy Saturday. Tami, Amy, Van, and Diego had already flipped through all the TV channels. They couldn't find anything worth watching.

"Let's play dominos," Van suggested.

"I have another idea," Diego said. "Let's play a game. We all like quiz shows. Why don't we make one up?"

"Good idea, Diego," Tami said. "Should we just make up some trivia questions?"

"I know!" Amy said. "We've been studying connotation and denotation in language arts class. Let's call our game 'What's the Difference?' The questions can be based on words that mean practically the same thing but bring different pictures to people's minds."

"Like what?" asked Diego. "Do you mean words like *heroes* and *heroines*?"

"No, heroes and heroines are really the same thing—you just use one word for males and the other for females. I mean words like *solos* and *performances*. They both mean some type of public presentation, but would you rather make solos or performances?"

"Performances," Diego replied promptly.

"That's because when I say *solos*, you think of performing by yourself with lots of people watching. *Performances* don't sound as pressured," Amy continued.

"I get it," said Tami. "I'll be the moderator, and you three can be the contestants. I'll ask a question, and the first one to knock on the table gets to answer it. The winner will be the one with the highest number of correct answers."

Everyone agreed to Tami's rules. Her first question was, "What's the difference between the words *gale* and *breeze*?"

Van knocked first. He said that both words describe how air can move, but that *breeze* has connotations of a gentle, pleasant wind, and *gale* has connotations of a strong, more unpleasant wind.

By 1:00, the score was exactly even. Amy, Van, and Diego all knew the connotations and denotations of words like *unusual* and *extraordinary*, *frigid* and *chilly*, and *nosy* and *inquisitive*. They also knew the differences between *aroma* and *odor*, *walk* and *strut*, *home* and *hut*, *oration* and *speech*, and *restaurant* and *diner*.

"Speaking of diners, I'm getting hungry," Amy said. "Look! It stopped raining. Let's go out and get something to eat."

"What is the difference between a hamburger and chopped steak?" asked Diego as they strolled toward the street—or was it a boulevard?

Checking Comprehension

1. Why did the four friends make up a quiz show?

   _____

2. Where do you think the story takes place? Explain your answer.

   _____

   _____

Practicing Comprehension Skills

Read each pair of words. Describe how their denotations are similar. Explain what their connotations suggest to you.

3. chilly/frigid

   _____

   _____

4. restaurant/diner

   _____

   _____

5. oration/speech

   _____

   _____

Read each of the following sentences. Then underline the word in parentheses that has the more positive connotation.

6. When the teacher finished his speech, the (nosy, inquisitive) student had many questions.

7. From the open restaurant door, the four friends could smell the wonderful (odor, aroma) of pizza.

8. Welcome to my cozy (home, hut).

Read the italicized words below each sentence. Then, on the line, rewrite
each group in order from the least strong to the strongest degree of meaning.
The first example has been done for you.

9. It was too _____cool, chilly, frigid_____ outside to ride bikes.

          chilly   frigid   cool

10. They could not take a walk because it was _____ .

          raining   sprinkling   pouring

11. The weather was _____ for that time of year.

          strange   unbelievable   extraordinary

12. It was _____ that the rain would stop soon.

          probable   likely   possible

Practicing Vocabulary

Write the word from the box that belongs with each group.

aroma	contestants	dismal	heroes	moderator	oration	solos

13. champions, winners, _____

14. participants, players, _____

15. single parts, perfomances, _____

16. fragrance, scent, _____

17. judge, referee, _____

18. gloomy, dreary, _____

19. speech, lecture, _____

Writing a Descriptive Paragraph
On another sheet of paper, write a paragraph describing an indoor game
or sport you enjoy playing. When you have finished, go back and circle
each word that has a positive connotation for you. Underline each word
that has a negative connotation.

Using a Map

Different features on a map are there to make the map easier for you to use. One standard feature found on most maps is a map **key**. The key lists special symbols, or pictures, and tells what each one stands for. Capitals and major routes are some of the features a key might show. The arrows on a **compass rose** show north, south, east, and west. The **scale** helps you estimate distances by showing a length on the map that is equal to a set number of miles or kilometers.

Not all maps give you the same information. **Road maps** display roads and highways. **Political maps** show boundaries such as state lines or the borders of countries. **Physical maps** show physical features of a land area such as rivers, valleys, and mountains. Other maps have special purposes, such as showing populations or industries.

Read the following paragraph. As you read, look at the map to help you understand what you read.

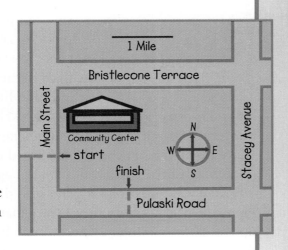

Carlos was thrilled. Today was the day of the race, and after training hard for weeks, he was ready. Excitedly, he traced the route in his mind. From the starting line on Main Street, he would jog north the first mile to Bristlecone Terrace. Then he would turn east at the community center and run two and a half miles. When he reached the corner at Stacey Avenue, he would make another right. Keeping up that pace for another mile and a half, he'd eventually see Pulaski Road. One more turn westward, and he could finally put on the speed. At that point, he'd have only a mile and a half to go until the finish line!

To turn east onto Bristlecone Terrace, which way did Carlos have to turn?

_____

In what direction is Carlos going when he runs along Stacey Avenue?

_____

Carlos runs the last mile and a half on what street?

_____

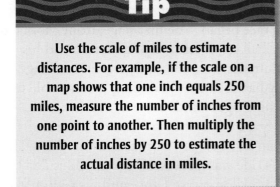

Tip

Use the scale of miles to estimate distances. For example, if the scale on a map shows that one inch equals 250 miles, measure the number of inches from one point to another. Then multiply the number of inches by 250 to estimate the actual distance in miles.

As you read the following article about Lance Armstrong's win in the 1999 Tour de France, refer to the map to help you visualize the route.

LANCE ARMSTRONG
AGAINST THE ODDS

Cancer can be one of the scariest words in the world. To Texas-born Lance Armstrong, a professional bicycle racer, it could have been a death sentence. At the very least, it could have been the end of his career—but it wasn't.

In 1996, at the age of 24, Lance learned he had a rare form of cancer that had spread to his brain and lungs. Doctors gave him only a 50-50 chance of recovery. After surgery and chemotherapy, Lance began his comeback. He pushed himself in training until he was winning races again. By 1999, he was ready to tackle the Tour de France, a grueling team bicycle race that goes up and down mountains and through hairpin turns in all kinds of weather. Think about bicycling 2,500 miles (about 4,000 kilometers) in 21 days!

The Tour is run in stages, or time periods. Lance won the qualifying race, and then the real race began. The first stage, from Montaigu to Challans, is relatively flat. Lance and his teammates were ahead. By the end of Stage 2, they had lost their lead. They weren't able to regain it again until Stage 8, in Metz.

Stage 9 was the first "mountain stage." It began in Le Grand Bornand, in the Alps. That day's ride was a course of about 132 miles (213.5 kilometers). Lance and his teammates pushed themselves as they had never done

before and enjoyed a six-minute lead as they reached the town of Sestrières.

Stage 9 was the turning point in the race. With a commanding lead, Lance and his team stayed ahead for the next eleven days. After pedaling through the Alps, they cycled through several stages that weren't too precipitous. Then came Stage 15, which began in Saint-Gaudens—the first of two days of climbing up the Pyrénées Mountains. The final stages took the team across western France and along the cobblestones of Paris's main avenue up to the finish line. Lance was the winner: the rider with the lowest time for all the stages overall. In 2000 this remarkable athlete again competed in the Tour de France—and once again, he won!

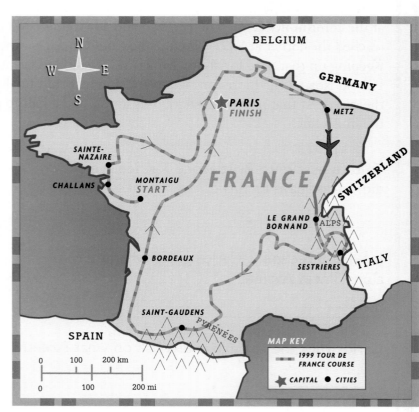

Checking Comprehension

1. Why is this selection entitled "Lance Armstrong: Against the Odds"?

    _____

    _____

2. What do you think Lance Armstrong is like as a person?

    _____

    _____

Practicing Study Skills

Use the map on page 132 to answer each question. Fill in the circle
next to the correct answer.

3. In which general direction did the cyclists ride from Le Grand Bornand
    to Sestrières?

    ○ northeast   ○ northwest   ○ southeast   ○ southwest

4. Through which of these cities did the cyclists go between
    Saint-Gaudens and the finish line in Paris?

    ○ Sestrières   ○ Metz   ○ Bordeaux   ○ Le Grand Bornand

5. If you could travel in a straight line from Paris to Metz, how far
    would you go?

    ○ about   ○ about   ○ about   ○ about
      600 miles   200 miles   5 miles   3,000 miles

6. In what part of France are the Pyrénées Mountains?

    ○ south   ○ northwest   ○ northeast   ○ east

7. Number the cities below from 1 to 4 in the order in which
    the 1999 Tour de France riders passed through them.

    _____ Metz   _____ Bordeaux   _____ Paris   _____ Saint-Gaudens

Using the map on page 132, write your answers to the following.

8. What is the capital of France? How do you know?

_____

9. Where is the country of Switzerland located in relation to France?

_____

10. The Pyrénées Mountains lie partly in France and partly in what other country of Europe?

_____

Practicing Vocabulary

Write the word from the box that belongs in each group.

commanding	grueling	precipitous	qualifying	relatively	scariest	surgery

11. strong, unbeatable, _____

12. exhausting, tiring, _____

13. steep, perpendicular, _____

14. medical procedure, operation, _____

15. somewhat, nearly, _____

16. most frightening, most terrifying, _____

17. determining, deciding, _____

Write a Journal Entry
Imagine that you just won an important race. On a separate sheet of paper, write a journal entry about it. Describe the race, the difficulties you encountered, and the way it felt to win. Include a small map to show the route of your race.

Understanding Charts and Tables

Have you ever traveled on a bus, train, airplane, or ship? All these forms of transportation run according to **schedules**. Most schedules show **departure times**, or the times the vehicle leaves, and **arrival times**, or the times it arrives.

Different schedules are organized in different ways and contain different information. The following schedule is arranged as a **timetable**—a special kind of table that presents information about arrivals and departures. To read a timetable, look at the headings, then read down the columns and across the rows to find the information you need.

Read the advertisement and the accompanying timetable. Notice how the timetable is set up. Use the advertisement and timetable to answer the following questions.

CRANBERRY POINT EXCURSION TRAIN
Daily Schedule**

Read down	Departures		
Cranberry Center	9:00 A.M.	1:00 P.M.	5:00 P.M.
Old Stone Bridge	9:30 A.M.	1:30 P.M.	5:30 P.M.
Cranberry Bay	10:30 A.M.	2:30 P.M.	6:30 P.M.
Cranberry Village*	11:45 A.M.	3:45 P.M.	7:45 P.M.

* The return to Cranberry Center takes 30 minutes

**Daily April–September; Saturdays, Sundays, & Holidays only, March & October; closed November–February

CRANBERRY POINT RAILROAD
Take a Scenic Journey Back in Time

Your family will enjoy a leisurely ride along the ocean peninsula to Cranberry Point. You'll have plenty of time to explore at stops in historic Cranberry Village, beautiful Cranberry Bay, and the unique Old Stone Bridge. Come ride with us!

Three departures daily from Edgar Station at Cranberry Center.

When are the "three departures daily" that are mentioned in the advertisement?

_____

How much time is there between the departure at Cranberry Bay and the departure at Cranberry Village?

_____

If you leave Cranberry Village at 7:45 P.M., what time will you arrive back at Cranberry Center?

_____

_____

Tip

All timetables are different, so look carefully to figure out departure and arrival times. Look for any notes and for symbols and the key that explains them.

On Your Own

As you read the passage, look at the timetable to find the information that is mentioned.

A Day at WESTORIA

"I vote for Dinosaur Park!" said Rob, reading the poster at the bus terminal. "I could stay there all day long." He was visiting his aunt, uncle, and cousin for the weekend, and the family had decided to sightsee at Westoria.

"It's essential that I see the crafts market," said Aunt Wilma.

"Attraction Number 5, Mystery Mine—that's where I want to go. I love mysteries!" Ellen said.

"I heard that the Museum of Rocks and Minerals is a real gem," said Uncle Otto jokingly. "But seriously, we need to look carefully at the bus schedule. We have to be realistic about how many attractions we can visit in one day if we plan to spend much time at each one."

"I'm sure that if we approach this creatively, we can figure something out to please each of us," said Aunt Wilma. Hastily, she added, "I see that Crafts Marketplace is the first stop. It's only half past eight now. We can take the nine o'clock bus."

"If I stay on that bus I'll be at Dinosaur Park in two hours," Rob said, studying the timetable.

"Each of us seems to have a different attraction in mind," said Uncle Otto. "What should we do?"

"How about if we split up?" suggested Ellen. "Dad and I can go to the museum and the mine. Mom and Rob can see the crafts and dinosaurs."

"That's a good compromise," said Uncle Otto as the others nodded agreeably. "At 4:45," he added, "we'll meet at Attraction Number 3 to soak our weary feet."

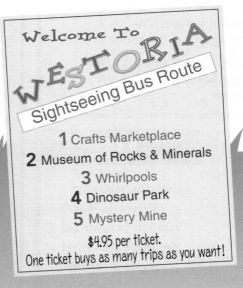

Welcome To **WESTORIA** Sightseeing Bus Route

1 Crafts Marketplace
2 Museum of Rocks & Minerals
3 Whirlpools
4 Dinosaur Park
5 Mystery Mine

$4.95 per ticket.
One ticket buys as many trips as you want!

Read Down To Attractions	Westoria Sightseeing Bus Timetable			
Terminal	9:00 A.M.	10:30 A.M.	12:00 P.M.	1:00 P.M.+
1 Crafts Marketplace	9:30 A.M.	11:00	12:30	1:30+
2 Museum of Rocks & Minerals	10:00	11:30	1:00	2:00+
3 Whirlpools	10:15	11:45	1:15	2:15+
4 Dinosaur Park	11:00	12:30 P.M.	2:00	3:00+
5 Mystery Mine	11:30	1:00	2:30	3:30+
To Terminal				
5 Mystery Mine	11:45 A.M.	1:30 P.M.	3:30 P.M.	4:30 P.M.+
4 Dinosaur Park	12:15 P.M.	2:00	4:00	5:00+
3 Whirlpools	1:00	2:45	4:45	5:45+
2 Museum of Rocks & Minerals	1:15	3:00	5:00	6:00+
1 Crafts Marketplace	1:45	3:30	5:30	6:30+
Terminal	2:15	4:00	6:00	7:00+
+ Saturdays and Sundays Only				

Checking Comprehension

1. What problem is the family trying to solve?

   _____

   _____

2. Do you agree that the family's solution is the best one?

   _____

   _____

Practicing Study Skills

Refer to the passage and the table to fill in the circle before the right answer.

3. The bus that leaves the Terminal at noon arrives in Dinosaur Park at 2:00 P.M.
   When does the next bus stop at that attraction?

   ○ one hour later   ○ two hours later   ○ six hours later   ○ half an hour later

4. At what time should Ellen and Uncle Otto leave the Museum of Rocks
   and Minerals to reach Attraction 5 at one in the afternoon?

   ○ 9:25 A.M.   ○ 9:30 A.M.   ○ 11:30 A.M.   ○ 12:30 P.M.

5. What is the latest bus that Ellen and Uncle Otto can take from the Mystery
   Mine to reach the Whirlpools by the agreed-upon time of 4:45?

   ○ 3:30 P.M.   ○ 2:30 P.M.   ○ 3:00 P.M.   ○ 4:00 P.M.

Refer to the passage and the tables to write the answers to these questions.

6. Rob and Aunt Wilma finish their tour of the Crafts Marketplace in two hours.
   Do they have time for lunch before boarding the bus to Dinosaur Park?
   Explain your answer.

   _____

   _____

7. How would the family have to change their plans if they visited Westoria on a weekday?

   _____

   _____

8. The family reached the whirlpools at 4:45. How much time did they have to spend there? Explain your answer.

_____

9. Complete the chart to show how the family could have visited four attractions in one day. In the last column, write the amount of time spent at each attraction.

Attraction	Arrive	Depart	Time Spent
1. Crafts Marketplace	9:30 A.M.	_____	_____
2. Museum of R & M	11:30	1:00 P.M.	_____
3. Whirlpools	_____	2:15	_____
4. Dinosaur Park	_____	5:00	_____

Practicing Vocabulary

Choose the word from the box that best completes each analogy. Write the word on the line.

10. unwanted : necessary :: useless : _____

11. crawl : slowly :: run : _____

12. frown : unhappily :: smile : _____

13. nap : sleep :: tired : _____

14. train : station :: bus : _____

15. paint : artistically :: think : _____

16. selfish : argue :: generous : _____

agreeably

compromise

creatively

essential

hastily

terminal

weary

Writing a Story
On another piece of paper, write a story in which transportation plays an important part. Create a table that will help readers keep track of the routes and times mentioned in your story.

Using Graphs

A **graph** gives you information as a picture. Writers often use graphs to make information in articles clearer. You are likely to find graphs as you read newspapers, magazines, and advertisements. Your science, math, and social studies books often use graphs, too.

Sometimes a graph's information appears in the form of a line or lines. A **line graph** can help you understand how something has changed over a period of time. Pay attention to the labels on the **horizontal** axis, or line at the bottom, and the **vertical** axis, or line at the left. They tell you what information is being presented.

Read this article on the weather pattern known as La Niña. Notice how the line graph helps you see how La Niña affects weather far away.

La Niña is part of the cycle of changing ocean temperatures known as El Niño. In a "La Niña" year, the average sea temperature in the central Pacific Ocean drops at least half a degree Celsius for six months or more. At the same time, winds from the west are quite strong. La Niña occurs every four to ten years.

La Niña affects weather in America. Winter weather in a "La Niña" year is usually cooler than usual in the northeast. In much of the southern U.S., however, the weather is warmer and drier.

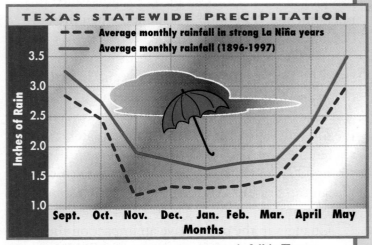

The graph above compares average rainfall in Texas overall with rainfall during strong "La Niña" years. Averages for each month from September through May are given for the period from 1896-1997.

Look at the graph. Answer the questions on the lines.

During the time period from 1896-1997, was there more or less rain in Texas during strong "La Niña" years? Explain your answer.

_____

_____

Look at the amount of rain in an average month of May in Texas compared to the amount of rain in a strong "La Niña" year. About how much less rainfall than the average can Texans expect in May of a strong "La Niña" year?

_____

Tip

When you read a line graph, the vertical axis and the horizontal axis will be labeled with information. Pay attention to these labels to know what information the graph presents.

Read the article about El Niño. Notice that the graph provides information that supports certain ideas in the article.

What Is El Niño?

For centuries the sailors of Peru noticed something that happened each December. The normally cool water along the coast was replaced by a warmer ocean current. Fish were harder to find in this part of the Pacific Ocean. The sailors called this phenomenon "El Niño." The period when these ocean waters were colder is called "La Niña."

In most years, the warming from El Niño is small. It lasts for only a few months and is confined to a narrow strip of ocean along the coast of Peru and Ecuador. Every four to seven years, however, the increase is pronounced. Near the equator, the sea temperature may rise by several degrees. In a strong El Niño year, much of the eastern Pacific Ocean can heat up. A strong El Niño can last for many months.

Changes in the ocean have an impact on the atmosphere. Because of this, a powerful El Niño has dramatic effects on the world's weather. Fierce rainstorms soak the coastal regions of Peru and Ecuador, causing floods. In southeast Asia and Australia, however, the same El Niño causes extremely dry weather. In Australia, droughts related to El Niño often cause wildfires.

El Niño also disrupts weather in the United States, especially in winter. People in the Northeast can thank El Niño if it feels like spring in January. To the Southeast and Gulf Coast, the phenomenon will probably bring more rain than normal. A moderate El Niño usually causes dry conditions in the western United States. A strong El Niño, by contrast, brings very wet weather there.

Predictions about El Niño can't be made easily. The same is true of La Niña, which is part of the same weather cycle as El Niño although it has an opposite effect on the world's weather. However, scientists do agree on how to measure El Niño and La Niña. They take the ocean's temperatures along part of the equator. If the temperature averages more than half a degree Celsius (.9 degrees Fahrenheit) above normal for at least six months, it's an El Niño year. If the temperature averages less than half a degree Celsius below normal, it's a La Niña year.

The graph shows changes in the average annual temperatures in Boston, Massachusetts, before and after the start of an El Niño cycle.

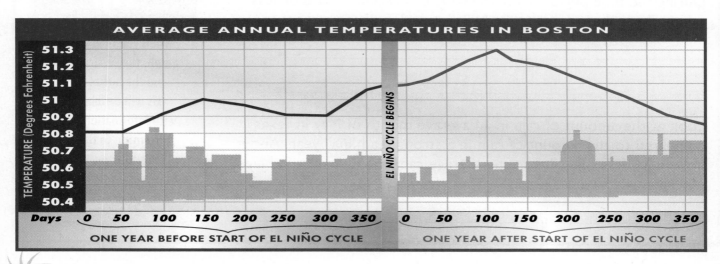

AVERAGE ANNUAL TEMPERATURES IN BOSTON

ONE YEAR BEFORE START OF EL NIÑO CYCLE · ONE YEAR AFTER START OF EL NIÑO CYCLE

Checking Comprehension

1. What is the difference between La Niña and El Niño?

_____

_____

_____

2. Why might people in the northeastern United States enjoy the effects of a strong El Niño more than people on the West Coast?

_____

_____

Practicing Study Skills

The graph on page 140 shows changes in average annual temperatures in Boston. It includes periods before and after the start of an El Niño cycle. The blue line shows average temperatures for a year before the start of an El Niño cycle. The red line shows average temperatures for a year after the start of an El Niño cycle.

Study the graph. Then fill in the circle next to the correct answer.

3. The graph shows that *following* the start of an El Niño cycle, temperatures in Boston:

   ○ usually stay exactly the same.   ○ rise by several tenths of a degree.

   ○ fall by about ten degrees.   ○ rise by about ten degrees.

4. *Before* the start of an El Niño cycle, annual temperatures in Boston:

   ○ average between about 0 and 32   ○ average between about 50.8 and 51.1
      degrees Fahrenheit.   degrees Fahrenheit.

   ○ average between about 50.4 and 51.3   ○ average between about 0 and 365
      degrees Fahrenheit.   degrees Fahrenheit.

5. Averaged over a year, the warmest temperatures in Boston occur:

   ○ about 120 days after the start of   ○ about a year after the start of
      an El Niño cycle.   an El Niño cycle.

   ○ about a year before the start of   ○ long after the El Niño cycle has ended.
      an El Niño cycle.

6. The La Niña cycle has a *cooling* effect on Boston temperatures. We could expect a graph showing average annual temperatures in Boston before and after the start of a La Niña cycle:

- ○ to dip down, instead of up, after the start of the cycle.
- ○ to be flat, showing no change.
- ○ to look exactly like the graph for an El Niño cycle.
- ○ to show temperatures on the horizontal axis and days on the vertical axis.

Look at the graph on page 140. Then write the answer on the line.

7. What information does the horizontal axis provide?

_____

8. What information does the vertical axis provide?

_____

Building Vocabulary

Choose the word from the box that best matches each definition.
Write the word on the line.

9. _____ an unusual event

10. _____ clearly marked

11. _____ disturbs

12. _____ simply

13. _____ limited

14. _____ almost certainly

15. _____ periods of very dry weather

confined

disrupts

droughts

easily

phenomenon

probably

pronounced

Writing a News Story
Write a news story about an unusual weather event or disaster. The event can be real or imaginary. You might describe a heat wave in winter, a flooding rainfall, or a record-breaking drought. Be sure to tell who, what, when, where, and why in your story. Then make a graph to give additional information about the story. Use another sheet of paper for your story and your graph.

Using a Dictionary

When you read, you may come across a word you don't know. You can find the meaning of the word in a **dictionary**. The words a dictionary lists are called *entry words*, and they appear in alphabetical order. *Guide words* at the top of each dictionary page tell you the first and last words that appear on that page.

Following each entry word, you will find the *pronunciation*, or way to say the word, and usually its *part of speech*, such as noun or verb. You will also find one or more *definitions* and sometimes *example sentences* that use the word in context. Many dictionary entries will include an *etymology*, or word history, as well.

Read this dictionary entry for the word *browse*.

guide words

entry word

pronunciation

definitions

brown ➤ brutish

browse (brouz) *verb* 1. to nibble at leaves, twigs, shoots, etc. [Cows like to *browse* in a grassy field.] 2. to look through something in a casual way [I'm going to *browse* in the shops on Main Street.] (probably from the Middle French word *brouts*, plural of *brout*, sprout)

etymology

example sentence

Which dictionary definition of *browse* is used in this sentence?

I needed to find out more about robots for a science report, so I decided to browse different websites about robots.

_____

Fill in the circle before the correct answer or answers.

Look back at the guide words for the definition of *browse*. Which of these words would you be most likely to find on the same dictionary page as browse?

○ brownie   ○ broom

○ brush   ○ bucket

According to the dictionary definition, from what language does the word *browse* probably come?

○ Old Latin   ○ Middle French

○ Greek   ○ Old Norse

Tip

To find a word quickly, use the guide words at the top of each dictionary page. Think about alphabetical order to find the guide words your word will fall between. When you find the right page, again use alphabetical order to find your entry word.

Read the following article about robots. Look for words from robot technology that are now familiar terms.

ROBOTS

The word *robot* describes an amazing variety of machines. *Robots* have various skills, sizes, and shapes. They have different levels of intelligence. When people hear the word *robot*, they often think of a human-like creation out of a science fiction movie. In reality, most robots do not look like humans but are machines designed to do specific jobs. Many are just "smart arms." Their only human-like parts are an arm and hand that can perform jobs.

Robots are hardier than humans in many ways. They can go where humans can't go and can do work that is dangerous or repetitive. They don't require air, food, water, or comfortable temperatures. For this reason, they are perfect for work in outer space, under the sea, or in hazardous places on Earth. Robots work tirelessly. They never need a lunch break!

A robot's brain is a computer that can be programmed to perform tasks. Actually, a robot is simply a computer that moves. Sensors collect information from the robot's surroundings and send it to the computer brain. The sensors work like a human's eyes, ears, nose, and skin. One of the commonest types of sensor is a small camera that acts as the robot's eyes.

The "body" of a robot is a mix of machinery, motors, and power sources. Humans can control the "body" in various ways. They might push buttons, tilt joysticks, move a computer mouse, or give verbal orders. The operator's signals sometimes travel through a cable. More often they are sent by remote control using radio waves.

Robots no longer live only in the world of science fiction. Modern robotics has produced all sorts of mechanical workers. They guard museums at night, run errands in hospitals, milk cows, and explore the universe. Many manufacturers have robotized their factories. A lawn equipment company has already invented a turtle-shaped "mobot" that mows grass. Maybe someday your personal "sewbot" will mend your clothes and a "cookbot" will make your meals!

Checking Comprehension

1. Why are robots better suited for certain jobs than humans are?

_____

_____

2. How are a robot's sensors like a human's sensory organs?

_____

_____

Practicing Study Skills

Use the dictionary entries to complete the following items.

robot ➤ rod

robot (rō´ bät) *noun* **1.** a machine, often imaginary, made to look and work like a human being **2.** any machine that can be programmed to perform and repeat tasks automatically **3.** a person who acts or works automatically, like a machine (from *robota,* meaning *forced labor,* first used in a play by Czech writer Karel Capek)

robotics (rō bä´ tiks) *noun* the science or technology of producing or using robots

robotize (rō´ bə tīz) *verb* **1.** to make something automatic, especially a factory process [The factory owner decided to *robotize* the assembly line.] **2.** to make somebody act in an automated, unemotional way; to turn (a person) into a robot

3. What is the difference between *robot, robotics,* and *robotize?* Include their parts of speech in your answer.

_____

_____

_____

_____

Look back at the guide words. Fill in the circles before all the words that answer the question.

4. Which of the following words might appear on the same dictionary page as *robot*?

○ rock   ○ roam   ○ robust   ○ rodent

Fill in the blanks on the lines provided.

5. The word *robot* comes from the term *robota*, which was first used in a Czech

_____ . It originally meant _____ . The part of the

dictionary entry that gives this word history is called the _____ .

On the lines provided, write an example sentence for each of the three definitions of the word *robot*.

6. Definition #1: _____

7. Definition #2: _____

8. Definition #3: _____

_____

Practicing Vocabulary

Choose the word from the box that completes each analogy.

9. eye : human :: _____ : robot

10. built : assembled :: instructed : _____

11. weaker : feebler :: stronger : _____

12. safe : secure :: risky : _____

13. unusual : interesting :: _____ : boring

14. houses : built :: machines: _____

15. biggest : smallest :: rarest: _____

commonest
designed
hardier
hazardous
programmed
repetitive
sensor

MAKING THE Reading AND Writing CONNECTION

Writing a Narrative Paragraph
Choose one of the following words and look it up in a dictionary.

    power   *program*   *sense*   *remote*   *signal*

You will find that the word has more than one meaning. Write a narrative paragraph in which you use two meanings of the word to tell a story.

Using an Encyclopedia

To do research for a report, you might first look in an **encyclopedia**. If you were looking for an article on the Olympic Games in a print encyclopedia, you would look in the volume whose guide letters include the letter O. The **guide words** at the top of each page will name the first and last **entries**, or articles, on the two pages. To use a CD-ROM or on-line encyclopedia, you would type "Olympic Games" into a search box.

If the entry you need is a long one, check its section **headings**. They describe what that section is about. After you read an article, check to see if any **cross-references** are given. Cross-references direct you to other encyclopedia articles about the subject. In a print encyclopedia, cross-references are at the end of an entry and are introduced with the words *See also*. If you come upon a cross-reference with parentheses, the words in parentheses are the title of a section heading—for example, *See also* **Winter Sports (Ice Hockey)**. CD-ROM or on-line encyclopedias have electronic links to cross-references.

Read this excerpt from an encyclopedia article on the Winter Olympics. Pay attention to the section heading and the cross-references.

guide words

Winter Olympics

entry words

Winter Olympics have been held since 1924. While many events make up the Winter Olympic Games, the events fall into only seven categories. These categories are bobsledding, luge, skating, ice hockey, curling, skiing, and biathlon.

section heading

Bobsledding

The first Olympic bobsledding race took place at the first Winter Olympics. The games were held in France in 1924. The first crews were made up of four people. In the 1932 Olympics in the U.S., races for two-person crews were added. Bobsled runs are at least 1,500 meters long (about 1,640 yards). They have 15–20 turns. The first run in the U.S. was built near Lake Placid, New York, for the 1932 Winter Olympics.

cross-references

See also **Bobsledding (History); Lake Placid, New York.**

What section heading is shown in this portion of the encyclopedia entry?

_____

Which cross-reference is to an article about the site of the first U.S. bobsled run?

_____

Tip

When you research a topic in an encyclopedia, use the section headings to find the exact information you want. Use cross-references to find more information.

As you read the following encyclopedia article titled "U.S. Olympic Women's Ice Hockey Team," pay attention to the section headings and the cross-references.

United States Olympic Women's Ice Hockey Team is the U.S. entry in a medal sport first played at the 1998 Winter Olympics.

History

For years, women ice hockey players and coaches from teams around the world petitioned the International Olympic Committee to be included in the Winter Olympics. Membership on women's teams climbed steadily upward. The first women's world championship was held in March 1990. Then, in 1992, the International Olympic Committee announced that it would include women's ice hockey as a medal sport. Women ice hockey players first competed in the Olympics in 1998, in Nagano, Japan.

World Championships Established Rivalry

The 1997 Women's World Championships in ice hockey served to qualify teams for the 1998 Olympic Games. The top five countries from that tournament were Canada, the U.S., Finland, China, and Sweden. Japan, as host country, would also compete at Nagano. The Canadian team had beaten the U.S. team in all four world championships since 1990. The U.S. team was runner-up each

time. Team USA knew they would face formidable competition in the 1998 Winter Olympics. They were determined to avoid another defeat by Canada.

Two Pioneers

The first U.S. Olympic Women's Ice Hockey Team included two pioneers in the sport. They were Karyn Bye and team captain Cammi Granato. When she was fourteen, Bye had played ice hockey on a boys' team in Wisconsin. She wore a jersey that read "K. L. Bye." In the 1998 Winter Games, the 26-year-old Bye would play forward and serve as alternate captain. Team captain Granato was already a seasoned pro. She had been voted the U.S.A. Women's Hockey Player of the Year in 1996.

Historic Game 6

A series of wins at Nagano moved Team U.S.A. toward an expected showdown with the Canadian team. Game 6 was the first gold medal game in the history of women's ice hockey. As expected, the Canadian and American women battled fiercely during the first period of the game. The score stayed at 0–0. In the second period, American forward Gretchen Ulion broke the tie with a goal. Toward the end of the third period, with the score 2–0, the Canadians scored their only goal. With just seconds remaining in the game, Sandra Whyte scored the American team's third and final goal. The final score was U.S. 3, Canada 1.

See also **Winter Olympics; Ice Hockey; Canada (Winter Sports).**

1998 Winter Olympics U.S. Women's Ice Hockey Results		
U.S. 5	China	0
U.S. 7	Sweden	1
U.S. 4	Finland	2
U.S. 10	Japan	0
U.S. 7	Canada	4
U.S. 3	Canada	1

Checking Comprehension

1. Why was winning the 1998 gold medal in ice hockey so important for the U.S. women's ice hockey team?

_____

_____

2. What factors might have caused the International Olympic Committee to agree to make women's ice hockey an Olympic sport?

_____

_____

Practicing Study Skills

Write your answers to these questions in the blanks.

3. How many section headings does this article contain? _____

List the section headings on the lines below.

4. _____

5. _____

6. _____

7. _____

8. How many cross-references appear at the end of this article? _____

Fill in the circle or circles next to the correct answer for each item.

9. Which cross-reference would you look up to find out more about the various events at the Winter Olympics Games?

   ○ Winter Olympics   ○ Ice Hockey

   ○ Canada (Winter Sports)   ○ Two Pioneers

10. Look at the table that goes with the article. Which country scored the highest number of goals in a game against the U.S.?

   ○ Japan   ○ Finland   ○ Canada   ○ Sweden

11. Which section or sections would you read if you wanted to find out if the U.S. team beat Canada?

○ the table showing game scores ○ Historic Game 6

○ Two Pioneers ○ Canada (Winter Sports)

12. Use the section headings in the article to write a brief summary of the entry "United States Olympic Women's Ice Hockey."

_____

_____

_____

_____

_____

_____

Practicing Vocabulary

Write a word from the box that belongs with each group.

13. experienced, capable, _____

14. in the direction of, nearer to, _____

15. requested, asked, _____

16. loss, failure, _____

17. council, advisory board, _____

18. higher, above, _____

19. difficult, fierce, _____

committee

defeat

formidable

petitioned

seasoned

toward

upward

Writing a Summary
Choose a sport to research in an encyclopedia. Use section headings in the article to write a summary of the information in the article. Then describe additional information you could find by using any cross-references. Write your summary on another sheet of paper.

LESSON 34

Using a Library Card Catalog/ the Internet

All libraries use systems to organize their books and magazines so that you can find them easily. You've probably used one system, the **card catalog**, many times. Some libraries have a print card catalog. This set of cards lists all the books in the library. It contains three sets of alphabetized cards: title, subject, and author cards. **Title** cards give you the book's title first. **Subject** cards list each nonfiction book by its subject. They give you the subject of the book first. **Author** cards give you the author's name first.

TITLE CARD

006/Pim   Virtual Reality
Pimentel, Ken.
Virtual Reality: through the
new looking glass
New York, McGraw-Hill, 1995
438 p. illus.

SUBJECT CARD

006/Pim   VIRTUAL REALITY
Pimentel, Kim.
Virtual Reality: through the
new looking glass
New York, McGraw-Hill, 1995
438 p. illus.

AUTHOR CARD

006/Pim   Pimentel, Kim.
Virtual Reality: through the
new looking glass
New York, McGraw-Hill, 1995
438 p. illus.

If your library uses a computerized catalog system, the search process is similar to using a card catalog. You must first decide whether to search the database by author, title, or subject. Then you type in your selection and look at the choices.

AUTHOR: Jefferis, David
TITLE: Cyber Space: virtual reality and the
    World Wide Web
PUBLISHED: New York, NY: Crabtree Pub., c 1999
    Paging: 32 pp.: ill. Notes: Includes index
CALL NUMBER: J004 JEF—J. Nonfiction—In

How does a catalog card or database lead you to a book on the shelf? If the book is fiction, the card or database will show an **F** or **Fic.** Books of fiction are arranged on the shelves alphabetically by author's last name. If a book is nonfiction, the card catalog or database will show its call number. This **call number,** made up of numbers and letters, appears on the spine of the book. The books are placed on the shelf in order of their call numbers.

Library call numbers are part of the *Dewey Decimal System*. This system classifies nonfiction books into ten main groups shown on the chart below.

Dewey Decimal System			
000-099	General Reference Works	500-599	Pure Science
100-199	Philosophy	600-699	Technology
200-299	Religion and Mythology	700-799	The Arts
300-399	Social Sciences	800-899	Literature
400-499	Language	900-999	General Geography and History

Write *author, title,* or *subject* to tell how you would search for each book in the library.

A novel by Virginia Hamilton _____

Books about opera _____

The book *Computer Games and How to Win Them* _____

A book about the Grand Canyon _____

Use the information you've just learned to help you complete the chart below.

What You Need	Where to look: Subject, Title, or Author	Call Number Section
A book of Greek myths	_____	_____
A book called *An Introduction to Sculpture*	_____	_____

Today, many students search the **Internet** for information. Online, you can use encyclopedias, atlases, almanacs, and magazines. In addition, thousands of organizations post information on their home pages. To find what you need, your computer has software called a *search engine*. Search engines that are programmed for students and young people are especially useful.

To start an Internet search, type in a keyword to describe what you're looking for. The search engine then finds articles that contain that word. Be careful, though. If your keyword is too broad, you'll get far too many listings that aren't useful. Looking though them all would be a waste of time.

You can refine, or narrow, your search by using a specific keyword or keywords. If you must research Monarch butterflies, for example, don't enter *insects* or *butterflies*. Instead, enter *Monarch butterflies*. Then all the listings will tell about the one species you need to know more about. You can also refine your search by entering more than one keyword. If you need to know where Monarch butterflies migrate, enter *monarch butterflies* and *migration*. Then only information with all those words will be listed. You can also use a phrase within quotation marks, such as *"migrating Monarch butterflies,"* to refine a search.

Read the following paragraph. Think about keywords you could enter in a search engine to find more information on the subjects mentioned.

Video games were created years before you were born, but they have come a long way in a short time. The first video game, *Pong*®, appeared in 1972. It was a very simple game similar to Ping-Pong. The screen was black and white, and the sounds were quite basic. Yet Pong was so successful that it started the video game industry. Nearly any video game you play today can be traced back to the success of Pong. In less than thirty years, we have gone from the simple game of Pong to 3-D virtual reality games that put players in the middle of the action.

Jake wants to learn more about the history of video games. When he used the keywords "video games," he got thousands of responses. How should he refine his search?

_____

What keywords might you use to search the Internet for information about amusement parks that feature virtual reality rides?

_____

Tip

When researching information in a library card catalog or on the Internet, think about what you already know and what you need to know. Then make your selection and look at your choices.

As you read this article about virtual reality, think about the subject areas you could look up to find out more about some of the ideas that are discussed.

VIRTUAL REALITY: THE LOOK OF THE FUTURE

Although the idea of virtual reality (VR) has been around for a long time, it has only become a common term in recent years. VR is easier to describe than to define. It is an artificial environment for your senses. You can view a VR environment on a computer screen by looking at a 3-D world. You can also have a complete "immersion" in an environment, using such devices as a data glove and a head-mounted display. If you saw the movie *Tron*, you saw "live" actors immersed in a VR environment: they were inside a video game.

Games, however, are only one side to virtual reality. VR has many useful applications. For example, the U.S. government uses VR for many aspects of training. Instead of sending armed forces recruits out on submarines or planes, which is risky and expensive, recruits can be trained in a room. There, trainees participate in a VR program, such as steering a ship or landing a plane on an aircraft carrier. NASA also uses VR to simulate space travel for astronauts in training. Local governments train employees with VR too. Police and firefighters use VR to teach trainees to handle different situations from traffic accidents to fires in high-rise buildings.

Virtual reality also has numerous uses outside the government. It is becoming

common for doctors to learn new surgical techniques using VR. The procedure can be introduced with no risk to a real patient. Airline companies can use VR to design new planes and train pilots to fly them. People who study weather use VR to simulate hurricanes, tornadoes, and other weather events so they can better understand them.

In the years ahead, science will depend on VR even more. Engineers will build virtual bridges. Astronomers will tour virtual galaxies. Scientists will look inside a virtual atom. If you want to study art or literature, VR will be there too. VR programs will take you through the great art museums and libraries of the world.

Checking Comprehension

1. Why is virtual reality used in job training?

   _____

   _____

2. How might virtual reality be important in the future?

   _____

Practicing Study Skills

Read each item. Think about words you might use in a database search by subject to find library books that would provide useful information. Write the words on the line.

3. how engineers use virtual reality in aircraft design _____

4. how filmmakers create special effects with computers _____

5. which search engines are most useful for kids surfing the Internet _____

Use the following card catalog card to answer questions 6-8. Write your answers on the line.

025.04GRA	Online Kids
	Gralla, Preston. Revised Edition
	Online Kids: a young surfer's guide to cyberspace
	NY, John Wiley & Sons, Inc., 1995, 1999
	276 p.

6. What type of card is this? _____

7. When were the two editions of the book published? _____

8. Based on its call number, *Online Kids* would be shelved with what category of books in the library? _____

Suppose you are planning some Internet searches. Look at each group of keywords below. Circle the most specific keywords in each group.

9. blue whale migrations   blue whales   whales and dolphins

10. weather   tornadoes   storms

Fill in the circle before the correct answer.

11. Denise wants to write a report about how virtual reality computer software is used in medical schools to help train doctors to perform surgical and other medical procedures. She is using the Internet to find information. Fill in the circle next to the search phrase that would probably bring the best results.

○ Virtual reality computer software ○ Surgical and medical procedures

○ Virtual reality medical education ○ Computerized training

Practicing Vocabulary

12. Complete the paragraph with words from the box. Write the word on the lines.

applications	becoming	environment	galaxies	immersion	introduced	trainees

Often we think of virtual reality as only a form of entertainment. Increasingly, however,

VR is _____ a useful educational tool. Virtual reality will have many

_____ when it comes to training doctors, pilots, and other specialists. Pilot

and astronaut _____ could learn to fly on the ground with VR. After having

been _____ to the basics in this way, they could begin training in the air more

safely. Just about any setting or _____ can be created with VR, including a com-

plete _____ in the artificial experience. So whether you become a submarine

commander or an astronaut traveling to distant _____ , you might get your

early training with virtual reality.

Writing a Summary
Using either a library card catalog or the Internet, do some research on the subject of virtual reality to help you brainstorm ideas about how VR could be put to use in a sixth-grade classroom. On a separate piece of paper, write a summary of your ideas.

Level F Glossary

A

abruptly (ə brupt′ lē) *adverb* suddenly, without warning

acquisition (ak′ wə zish′ ən) *noun* something gained

admiration (ad′ mər ā′ shən) *noun* a feeling of delight and approval for beauty, skill, or other pleasing qualities

adorable (ə dôr′ ə bəl) *adjective* very attractive and likable

agreeably (ə grē′ ə blē) *adverb* in a pleasing or pleasant way

aloof (ə lo͞of′) *adjective* keeping oneself apart or at a distance

alternate (ôl′ tər nit) *noun* a person or thing that takes the place of another if needed; substitute

altitude (al′ tə to͞od) *noun* the height of a thing above Earth's surface or above sea level

antisocial (an′ ti so′ shəl) *adjective* not liking to be with other people

aperture (ap′ ər chər) *noun* opening; gap; hole

appalling (ə pôl′ iŋ) *adjective* shocking or horrifying

appears (ə pirz′) *verb* has the look of being; seems

applications (ap′ li ka′ shənz) *noun* acts of putting something to use

aroma (ə rō′ mə) *noun* a pleasant smell; fragrance

attempts (ə tempts′) *noun* tries or attacks

authentic (ô then′ tik or ä then′ tik) *adjective* genuine; real

B

ballast (bal′ əst) *noun* heavy material that is carried in a ship, balloon, or vehicle to keep it steady

basking (bask′ iŋ) *verb* staying in a warm, pleasant place

becoming (bē kum′ iŋ) *verb* coming to be

bisected (bī sekt′ əd or bī′ sekt əd) *verb* cut into two parts

brainchild (brān′ chīld′) *noun* someone's idea or invention

brooded (bro͞od′ əd) *verb* kept thinking in a troubled way

brutal (bro͞ot′ l) *adjective* cruel and without feeling; savage

C

camaraderie (kä′ mə rä′ dər ē) *noun* friendliness and loyalty among fellow workers

candidate (kan′ di dāt or kan′ di dət) *noun* a person who seeks a political office or an honor

captivated (kap′ tə vāt əd) *verb* attracted; interested

captures (kap′ chərz) *verb* represents or records in lasting form

catapulted (kat′ ə pult əd) *verb* threw with great force

challenging (chal′ ənj iŋ) *adjective* calling for skill or effort

chaotic (kā ät′ ik) *adjective* very confused or disordered

chided (chīd′ əd) *verb* found fault with; blamed

chivalry (shiv′ əl rē) *noun* the qualities that a knight was supposed to have, including courage and politeness

circuit (sʉr′ kət) *noun* a course around an area

circular (sʉr′ kyə lər) *adjective* having the shape of a circle

classic (klas′ ik) *adjective* of the highest quality or rank

comical (käm′ i kəl) *adjective* funny or amusing

commanding (kə mand′ iŋ) *adjective* powerful

committed (kə mit′ əd) *verb* pledged or promised

committee (kə mit′ ē) *noun* a group of people who are chosen to do something

commonest (käm′ ən ist) *adjective* most often seen or heard

complex (käm pleks′ or käm′ pleks) *adjective* made up of parts connected in a way that is hard to understand

composed (kəm pōzd′) *adjective* calm or peaceful

composers (kəm pō′ zərz) *noun* people who compose music

compromise (käm′ prə mīz) *noun* an ending of an argument brought about by each side giving up something

confined (kən fīnd′) *verb* kept within limits

confounds (kən foundz′) *verb* throws into confusion

congestion (kən jes′ chen) *noun* overcrowding; clogging

contestants (kən test′ əntz) *noun* people who take part in a contest

conversion (kən vʉr′ zhən) *noun* the act or process of converting, or changing; change

cordial (kôr′ jəl) *adjective* warm and friendly

counterproductive (kount′ ər prə duk′ tiv) *adjective* producing results opposite to the desired ones

cowering (kou′ ər iŋ) *verb* crouching in fear or shame

creatively (krē āt′ iv lē) *adverb* in an imaginative way

critical (krit′ i kəl) *adjective* important to the outcome of a situation

crucial (kro͞o′ shəl) *adjective* of the greatest importance; needed in order to decide something

culmination (kul′ mə nā′ shən) *noun* the most important phase or stage; peak

cultivate (kul′ ti vāt) *verb* to grow from seeds or other plant parts

D

defeat (dē fēt′) *noun* failure to win

defender (dē fend′ ər) *noun* someone who acts, speaks, or writes in support of another person

deflate (di flāt′) *verb* to let air or gas out of an object

delay (dē lā′) *noun* the act of putting off to a later time

descend (dē send´) *verb* to move down to a lower place

deserted (dē zʉrt´ əd) *adjective* abandoned; empty of people

designed (dē zīnd´) *verb* set apart for a certain use

destination (des´ ti nā´ shən) *noun* the place that a person or thing is going to

devoured (dē vourd´) *verb* ate up in a hungry way

disappointment (dis ə point´ ment) *noun* feeling that something wanted, expected, or promised failed to happen

disapproves (dis ə pro͞ovz´) *verb* has a feeling against

disguises (dis gīz´ əz) *noun* things used to hide a person's identity

dismal (diz´ məl) *adjective* dark and gloomy

disrupts (dis rupts´) *verb* interrupts the orderly progress of

distractions (dis trak´ shənz) *noun* things that draw away the mind or attention to something else

distributed (dis trib´ yo͞ot əd) *verb* gave out in portions

diversions (di vʉr´ zhənz or dī vʉr´ zhənz) *noun* things that a person turns to for fun in order to relax; pastimes

donned (dänd) *verb* put on clothing

droughts (drouts) *noun* long periods of dry weather

E **earnestness** (ʉr´ nəst nəs) *noun* seriousness or sincerity

earthly (ʉrth´ lē) *adjective* having to do with life on earth

easily (ē´ zi lē) *adverb* without trying too hard

electronics (ē lek´ trän´ iks or el´ ek trän´ iks) *noun* the science that deals with the action of electrons and their use in devices

embellished (em bel´ isht) *verb* made a story more interesting with fictional additions

emperor (em´ pər ər) *noun* a person who rules an empire

encounter (en koun´ tər) *verb* to meet unexpectedly

enthusiasm (en tho͞o´ zē az´ əm) *noun* a strong interest

environment (en vī´ rən mənt) *noun* all the things and conditions that surround a person, animal, or plant

essential (ē sen´ shəl) *adjective* most important or necessary

estimated (es´ ti māt´ əd) *verb* made a general but careful guess about the size, quality, value, or cost of

exceptional (ek sep´ shə nəl) *adjective* outstanding

exhausted (eg zôst´ əd or eg zäst´ əd) *verb* made very tired

experiments (ek sper´ i mənts) *noun* tests that are used to find out or prove something

explanation (eks´ plə nā´ shən) *noun* something that shows the meaning of; reason

exposing (eks pōz´ iŋ) *verb* causing to know about or experience

F **facial** (fā´ shəl) *adjective* having to do with the face

familiar (fə mil´ yər) *adjective* well-known

fascination (fas´ i nā´ shən) *noun* a very strong interest

focus (fō´ kəs) *verb* to adjust the eye or a lens in order to make a clear image

footsore (fo͝ot´ sôr´) *adjective* having feet that hurt from much walking

formally (fôr´ mə lē) *adverb* in a way that follows usual rules or customs exactly

formidable (fôr´ mə də bəl) *adjective* hard to overcome

friction (frik´ shən) *noun* the force that slows the motion of two surfaces that touch each other

G **gadgets** (gaj´ əts) *noun* small, mechanical devices

galaxies (gal´ ək sēz) *noun* very large groups of stars

grave (grāv) *adjective* dignified; solemn

grimaced (gri māst´ or grim´ əst) *verb* twisted the muscles of the face to express pain or unhappiness

grueling (gro͞o´ əl iŋ) *adjective* very tiring; exhausting

H **happiness** (hap´ ē nəs) *noun* the condition of being happy

hardier (har´ dē ər) *adjective* more capable of surviving under bad conditions; stronger

hastily (hās´ ti lē) *adverb* quickly; in a hurry

hazardous (haz´ ər dəs) *adjective* dangerous

hedged (hejd) *verb* avoided giving a direct answer

helm (helm) *noun* the wheel or tiller by which a ship is steered

heroes (hir´ ōz or hē´ rōz) *noun* people who are looked up to

hikers' (hīk´ ərz) *adjective* belonging to people who take long walks, especially in the country or in woods

huddled (hud´ əld) *verb* crowded or pushed close together

hull (hul) *noun* the sides and bottom of a boat or ship

humidity (hyo͞o mid´ i tē) *noun* the amount of moisture in the air

hurtles (hʉrt´ əlz) *verb* moves with great speed or force

I **illuminate** (i lo͞o´ mi nāt´) *verb* give light to; light up

immersion (i mʉr´ zhən) *noun* the state of getting deeply involved or absorbed in

immigrants (im´ i grənts) *noun* people who come into a country to make a new home

immigrants (im´ i grənts) *noun* people who come into a country to make a new home

improvise (im´ prə vīz) *verb* to make up and perform at the same time, without preparation

impulsively (im pul´ siv lē) *adverb* without thinking

infancy (in´ fən sē) *noun* the earliest stage of something

influence (in´ flōō əns) *noun* the power to act on or affect persons or things in ways that are either good or bad

ingredients (in grē´ dē ənts) *noun* the things that make up a mixture

instantaneously (in´ stən tā´ nē əs lē) *adverb* in an instant

instinct (in´ stiŋkt) *noun* a way of behaving that is natural to an animal or person from birth

interior (in tir´ ē ər) *noun* the inside or inner part

Internet (in´ tər net) *noun* a network of computers from around the world that are connected for sharing information

introduced (in trə dōōst´) *verb* brought into use

irritable (ir´ i tə bəl) *adjective* easy to anger or annoy

L
lax (laks) *adjective* not strict; careless

legendary (lej´ ən der´ ē) *adjective* having to do with a legend

leisurely (lē´ zhər lē) *adverb* without hurry

leveled (lev´ əld) *verb* knocked to the ground

liberty (lib´ ər tē) *noun* being free from control

lifeboats (līf´ bōts) *noun* sturdy boats used for saving lives at sea or along the shore

log (lôg) *noun* the record of a trip or voyage

luxurious (lug zhōōr´ ē əs) *adjective* giving a feeling of comfort and pleasure

M
magnitude (mag´ ni tōōd) *noun* great size

maintaining (mān tān´ iŋ) *verb* keeping or keeping up

melodies (mel´ ə dēz) *noun* series of musical tones that make up tunes

merciless (mɥr´ si ləs) *adjective* without pity; cruel

midpoint (mid´ point) *noun* the place in the exact middle

miserable (miz´ ər ə bəl) *adjective* very unhappy; sad

mission (mish´ ən) *noun* a special duty or piece of work that a person or a group is sent out to do

moderator (mäd´ ə rā´ tər) *noun* person in charge of a discussion or debate

monotonous (mə nät´ n əs) *adjective* having little change; boring

N
nature's (nā´ chərz) *adjective* belonging to the physical world

nutrition (nōō trish´ ən) *noun* food; nourishment

O
obscuring (äb skyōōr´ iŋ) *verb* hiding from view

obtain (äb tān´) *verb* to get through effort

obvious (äb´ vē əs) *adjective* easy to see or understand; clear

occasionally (ō kā´ zhə nə lē) *adverb* once in a while

optional (äp´ shən əl) *adjective* allowing one to make a choice; not required

oration (ô rā´ shən) *noun* a formal public speech delivered on a special occasion

overhead (ō´ vər hed) *adjective* above one's head

overjoyed (ō vər joid´) *adjective* very happy; delighted

overwhelming (ō vər hwelm´ iŋ) *adjective* overcoming completely

P
parachutist (per´ ə shōō´ tist) *noun* a person who jumps from an aircraft using a parachute

parcel (pär´ səl) *noun* a wrapped package; a bundle

peal (pēl) *noun* a loud sound that echoes

peculiar (pi kyōōl´ yər) *adjective* odd or strange

permitting (pər mit´ iŋ) *verb* giving consent to; allowing

perspective (pər spek´ tiv) *noun* a certain point of view in understanding or judging things

petitioned (pə tish´ ənd) *verb* made a serious written request

phenomenon (fə näm´ ə nän) *noun* an unusual person or thing

placidly (plas´ id lē) *adverb* calmly and quietly; peacefully

platform (plat´ fôrm) *noun* all the plans and goals of a political candidate or party

poorly (pōōr´ lē) *adverb* badly; not well

precipitous (pri si´ pə təs) *adjective* very steep, perpendicular

pried (prīd) *verb* released by force

probably (präb´ ə blē) *adverb* almost certainly

programmed (prō´ gramd) *verb* given a set of instructions

pronounced (prō nounst´) *adjective* clearly marked; definite

propels (prō pelz´) *verb* pushes or drives forward

prosperous (präs´ pər əs) *adjective* successful or thriving

provoked (prō vōkt´) *verb* annoyed or made angry

pupil (pyōō´ pəl) *noun* the opening in the center of the eye

pursuit (pər sōōt´ or pər syōōt´) *noun* the act of chasing after someone or something

Q **qualifying** (kwäl´ i fi´ iŋ) *verb* proving fit for some activity

R **recap** (rē kap´) *verb* to review by a brief summary

relatively (rel´ ə tiv lē) *adverb* compared to something else

remote (rē mōt´) *adjective* far off from a particular place

repaired (rē perd´) *verb* put into good condition again; fixed

repetitive (ri pet´ ə tiv) *adjective* repeating; saying or doing something again

resentfully (rē zent´ fə lē) *adverb* with a feeling of bitter hurt

retina (ret´ n ə) *noun* the inner layer of the lining of the eyeball

retrieved (rē trēvd´) *verb* found and brought back

reusable (rē yo͞o´ zə bəl) *adjective* capable of being used again

reviewed (rē vyo͞od´) *verb* went over or studied again

roaming (rōm´ iŋ) *verb* traveling about with no special purpose

S **scariest** (sker´ ē əst) *adjective* causing the most fear

scrumptious (skrump´ shəs) *adjective* delicious

seasoned (sē´ zənd) *adjective* better because of age or experience

sensor (sen´ sər) *noun* device that reacts to heat, light, pressure, etc.

serene (sə rēn´) *adjective* calm or peaceful

shelves (shelvz) *noun* thin, flat pieces of a material that are fastened against a wall or built into a frame so as to hold things

shifted (shif´ təd) *verb* changed from one position to another

shrewd (shro͞od) *adjective* clever or sharp in practical matters

signatures (sig´ nə chərz) *noun* people's names written by those people

sites (sīts) *noun* places on the Internet that have information on specific topics

smokejumper (smōk´ jum´ pər) *noun* a firefighter who parachutes to forest fires

solitary (säl´ i ter´ ē) *adjective* living or being alone

solos (sō´ lōz) *noun* performances by one person alone

somber (säm´ bər) *adjective* dark and gloomy or dull

spectacularly (spek tak´ yə lər lē) *adverb* in a showy way

stampeded (stam pēd´ əd) *verb* moved in a sudden rush of animals or people in one direction

steamship (stēm´ ship) *noun* a ship that is powered by steam

subway (sub´ wā) *noun* an underground railway that is usually powered by electricity

succinctly (sək siŋkt´ lē) *adverb* in few words; briefly

superheated (so͞o´ pər hēt´ əd) *adjective* heated to an extreme degree or to a very high temperature

superstitious (so͞o´ pər stish´ əs) *adjective* influenced by fearful beliefs

surgery (sʉr´ jər ē) *noun* the treating of disease or injury by cutting into and removing or repairing parts of the body

survivors (sər vīv´ ərz) *noun* people or things that survive

suspended (sə spend´ əd) *verb* stopped for a time

T **technology** (tek näl´ ə jē) *noun* science as used in everyday life

tenacity (ti nas´ ə tē) *noun* persistence in working toward a goal

terminal (tʉr´ mi nəl) *noun* a main station

thieves (thēvz) *noun* people who steal in a secret way

tiresome (tīr´ səm) *adjective* tiring; boring; annoying

toward (tôrd or twôrd) *preposition* in the direction of

trainees (trā nēz´) *noun* people who are receiving training

tutor (to͞ot´ ər) *verb* to act as a private teacher

U **unidentified** (un´ i den´ ti fīd) *adjective* not known or recognized

upward (up´ wərd) *adverb* from a lower to a higher place

urging (ʉrj´ iŋ) *verb* encouraging strongly

ushered (ush´ ərd) *verb* showed the way or brought in

V **vaguely** (vāg´ lē) *adverb* in a way that is unclear

versus (vʉr´ səs) *preposition* in a contest against

visual (vizh´ o͞o əl) *adjective* having to do with sight or used in seeing

vital (vīt´ l) *adjective* very important

voice-over (vois´ ō´ vər) *noun* the voice of an offscreen narrator, announcer, or character

W **weary** (wir´ ē) *adjective* tired

wilderness (wil´ dər nəs) *noun* a wild area; land that has no settlers and is covered with wild plants and trees

wispy (wis´ pē) *adjective* thin; slight

wistfully (wist´ fə lē) *adverb* with a feeling of longing

worthy (wʉr´ thē) *adjective* deserving; having merit